Granville County

North Carolina

Granville County

North Carolina

LOOKING BACK

LEWIS BOWLING

Charleston   London

History
PRESS

Published by The History Press
Charleston, SC 29403
www.historypress.net

Front cover: The Oxford High School Band parades down College Street in Oxford.
Back cover: Bicyclists gather on Main Street in Oxford in 1897. *Photo courtesy of Richard Thornton Library*.

All photos are courtesy of the author unless otherwise noted.

First published 2007

Manufactured in the United Kingdom

ISBN 978.1.59629.333.5

Library of Congress CIP data applied for.

*To my wife Beth, the best teacher in all of Granville County,
and the love of my life.*

Contents

CONTENTS

Introduction

Welcome to Granville County

There is a place I know that has made historic contributions to our state and country.

This place is full of intriguing people and notable events that have made it what it is today.

This place can be proud of a man who was the chief administrator of our nation's space program shortly before we landed on the moon.

It can be proud of a signer of the Declaration of Independence.

This place produced a Rhodes Scholar, who later became the chancellor of the University of North Carolina at Chapel Hill.

At one time, one of the most respected colleges for women in the state could be found within its borders.

One of its springs produced water that was sold throughout America and Europe.

Two of the finest orphanages exist here, both serving in a vital capacity for more than one hundred years.

Rochester, New York, is named after one of its citizens.

A county in Texas is named after one of its former residents.

It is proud to be home of the only African American to serve in the United States Congress from 1889 to 1890.

It has a tobacco heritage second to none, and two brothers who called this place home introduced flue-cured tobacco to Canada.

One of its towns was one of three finalists for the site of the University of North Carolina at Chapel Hill, and of this university's first sixteen graduates, four were from this section of the state.

One of its towns was considered the mule-trading capital of America.

A military training center was built here, which played an important role in our victory in World War II.

Bumper-to-bumper traffic heads down College Street in Oxford ca. 1920. *Photo courtesy of Ernestine Pruitt.*

One of its young athletes became an All-American football player at Duke University and went on to play in the National Football League.

One of its authors was a prolific writer of textbooks, one received our state's highest literary award and one sold more than six million books worldwide.

Are you a fan of *The Andy Griffith Show*? Well, a gentleman from this place wrote many of the scripts for the program.

Just where is this land of such rich history?

This place is our home, Granville County.

Our county has had its triumphs and glory days, and its share of growing pains, missteps and tragedies. It is a county we should cherish, for its past will help guide us as we continue to make Granville such a wonderful place to live.

Hopefully I have piqued your curiosity enough that you will want names and answers to these events that took place in our county. Well, here goes:

James Webb was administrator of America's space program from 1961 to 1968, leading the effort to our landing on the moon in 1969. James also had a well-known father, John Frederick Webb, for whom J.F. Webb High School is named.

John Penn, who owned a plantation in Stovall, was a signer of the Declaration of Independence.

Ferebee Taylor went from Oxford High School to Oxford University in England on a Rhodes scholarship, and later became chancellor of the University of North Carolina at Chapel Hill.

Oxford Female College graduated more than five thousand young ladies.

Buckhorn Mineral Springs in Bullock produced fine-tasting water that was sold throughout the world. A customer in 1906 wrote, "While in Savannah, Georgia, I saw in a store several bottles of your spring water standing on the counter. Inquiry led me to try one bottle. It has brought a great change to my whole body. I feel much as I did at the age of twenty-five. I am now sixty-seven. The old machine is good yet, thanks to Buckhorn Water." It makes me wish those bottles were still on store shelves now!

Of course, the great service provided by the Central Children's Home and the Masonic Home for Children, both of Oxford, is well documented.

Rochester, New York, is named for Nathaniel Rochester of Granville County, and a county in Texas is named for Robert Potter of Granville.

Henry Cheatham was the only African American United States congressman from 1889 to 1890, and later served as a superintendent of the Central Children's Home.

Early in our county's history, Williamsboro was considered a possible site for our nation's first public university, UNC-CH., and Granville gave UNC four of its first sixteen graduates.

Creedmoor was once the center of mule trading, and Camp Butner played a vital role during World War II.

Ed Meadows won many accolades while playing football at Oxford High School, later becoming an All-American at Duke and a star player in the NFL.

Frank Slaughter, of Berea, sold millions of his novels, many of which can be found on the shelves of the Richard H. Thornton Library in Oxford. Henry Patillo and Thad Stem were also very accomplished authors.

Edgar Patrick authored a book about horses, which features a Granville horse named Black Snake. Black Snake was one of the fastest horses in the country in the 1820s. In fact, Granville at one time had horse racetracks.

Educators such as John Chavis, G.C. Credle, the Horners of Horner Military Academy and Sallie Mae Ligon and Thomas Currin of the Masonic Home for Children have all contributed so much to Granville County.

If you enjoy the antics of Andy and Barney on *The Andy Griffith Show*, as I do, we should give thanks to Harvey Bullock of Oxford, who wrote many of the scripts.

Pretty impressive history, is it not?

Granville County Timeline

1700   American Indians live in Granville County, including the Sapona, Tuscarora and Occanechi.

1701   John Lawson travels through what is now Granville, calling the land the "Flower of Carolina" for the fertility of the land.

1728   William Byrd surveys the area now known as Granville County, and notes the abundance of game, including deer, bear and buffalo.

1746   Granville County is established and derives its name from Lord John Carteret, known as the Earl of Granville.

1759   Granville Land Riots occur, resulting from questions of the Earl of Granville's legal rights to land in the area.

1760   Thomas Person purchases two hundred acres of land, and on it he builds a plantation known as Oxford.

1774   Granville citizens express their intent to revolt against English rule in the "General Meeting of Freeholders."

1776   Thomas Person of Granville is on the committee to draft North Carolina's constitution. John Penn of Stovall signs the Declaration of Independence.

1788   Nutbush Seminary, later named Williamsboro Seminary, is founded.

Walter and Ida Bullock are headed to church.

1805 John Chavis of Granville County opens a classical school in Raleigh; Bost Gooch of Stem invents the crossweave tobacco basket on which tobacco was stacked on the warehouse floor. Gooch also invents the first plow made of iron used in America, called Gooch's Twist.

1811 Oxford Male Academy and Oxford Female Academy are chartered; Nathaniel Rochester of Granville County founds Rochester, New York.

1816 Oxford is incorporated.

1840 Tobacco is established as the staple crop of Granville, producing 3,912,822 pounds, more than any other county in the state; the Raleigh and Gaston Railroad is completed, a track which runs through Granville County and helps farmers market their product outside of the county and state; the Oxford Courthouse is completed.

1842 Robert Potter, a former resident of Granville County, dies. A Texas county is named for Potter, who served Texas as secretary of the navy.

1851   Oxford Female College is formed.

1855   Horner Military Academy is formed.

1857   St. John's College is chartered.

1861   There are over ten thousand slaves in Granville County.

1861–   Fifteen hundred men serve our nation in the War Between the
1865   States, including the Granville Grays.

1866   The first warehouse in Granville County is built by Dr. L.C
        Taylor.

1873   Oxford Orphanage opens.

1881   Oxford's first railroad is completed; *Oxford Public-Ledger* is
        established.

1887   Central Children's Home opens; a huge fire destroys half of the
        business district in downtown Oxford.

1888   Mary Potter School opens.

1889–   Henry Cheatham serves in the United States Congress, later
1893   serving as superintendent of the Central Children's Home.

Early   The Gregory brothers, William and Francis, introduce flue-
1900s   cured tobacco to Canada.

1904   Buckhorn Mineral Springs is discovered.

1905   Creedmoor is incorporated.

1911   C.G. Credle opens; Oxford Tobacco Research Station opens,
        becoming the largest tobacco research facility in the world.

1913   Tiny Broadwick, born in Creedmoor, becomes the first woman
        to parachute from an airplane. Over sixty thousand people
        witness her jump at Griffith Park in Los Angeles.

1916   Streets of Oxford are paved.

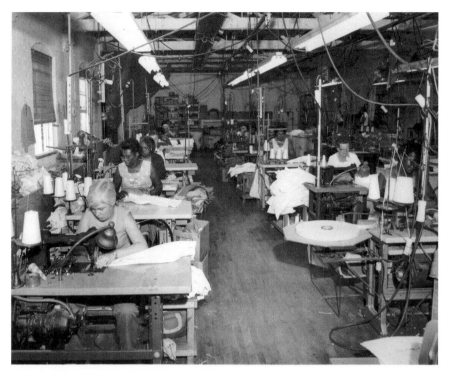

Above: Some ladies are hard at work in an Oxford Factory.

Below: Pictured left to right are Roy Breedlove, Paul Daniel and William Smith in the Granville Locker Plant. *Photo courtesy of Elaine Breedlove.*

1917–
1918	Many Granville County citizens participate in World War I.

1926	Over fifteen million pounds of tobacco are produced in Granville County; Lee Meadows of Oxford leads major league baseball in wins as a pitcher, with twenty, playing for the Pittsburgh Pirates.

1927	Hotel Oxford is built.

1932	Hoover Cart Rodeo is held in Oxford during Depression, attracting fifteen thousand spectators.

1936	G.C. Hawley High School opens for African American students.

1938	Granville Hospital opens.

1941	Frank Slaughter, from Berea and a graduate of Oxford High School, writes his first book, *That None Should Die.* Slaughter goes on to become a nationally renowned writer.

1941–
1945	World War II occurs, involving many Granville County citizens.

1942	Camp Butner opens.

1946	Bicentennial Celebration of Granville County is observed.

1952	Ed Meadows wins All-American status in football playing for Duke University. Meadows goes on to star in the NFL.

1964	Richard Thornton Library opens in its current location.

1965	*Butner-Creedmoor News* is established.

1969	Man lands on the moon. James Webb, from Oxford, serves as administrator of National Aeronautics and Space Administration from 1961 to 1968—Webb is a major force behind the moon landing.

1970	A young black man, Henry Marrow, is killed, creating racial tensions in Oxford and the surrounding areas.

1971	Oxford-Henderson Airport is built.

1972   Interstate 85 passes through Granville County; Oxford native Ferebee Taylor is named chancellor of the University of North Carolina at Chapel Hill, and serves until 1980.

1974   Thad Stem receives the North Carolina Literature Award.

1976   Vance Granville Community College opens.

1980s Major manufacturing companies move to Granville County.

1982   Sam Ragan of Berea is named North Carolina Poet Laureate by Governor Jim Hunt.

2003   The population of Granville County is 51,852.

2005   Creedmoor celebrates its one hundredth birthday.

2007   Granville County native Richard Moore announces candidacy for governor of North Carolina; Granville Central High School opens; Butner is incorporated as a town of Granville County.

2008   New John Umstead Hospital opens.

Oxford

4, March 1812—Thomas B. Littlejohn of Granville Co. to Robert Burton, Charles Eaton, John Hare, Robert Jeter, Benjamin Hilliard, Commissioners in trust for the trust for the county of Granville $2,636.00 by virtue of an act of the General Assembly of the State of North Carolina passed at Raleigh in the session of 1811 entitled an act to appoint Commissioners to contract with Thomas B. Littlejohn for fifty acres of Land to erect a Town…the said Robert Burton, Charles Burton, John Hare, Robert Jeter, and Benjamin Hilliard were appointed Commissioners to carry the said act being a part of the tract of Land called the Court House or Oxford tract…beginning…near where the former Jail stood, ninety feet from the west end of the Court House designated in the annexed plan by the letter A…

That is how the town of Oxford got started. In 1760, Samuel Benton acquired title to two hundred acres of land, which he called "Oxford Plantation." Eventually Thomas Littlejohn bought some of this land, and Granville County bought fifty acres from Littlejohn, as described above. Littlejohn developed lots around the present courthouse and established a hotel himself. The town began to grow and expand slowly. In 1830, the first local newspaper, the *Oxford Examiner*, was established. In 1840, the Granville County Courthouse was completed, and this building remains the center of Oxford today. By 1850, there were 669 people in Oxford. Agriculture has, through the years, been the driving force of the economy in Oxford and the county, with tobacco being the main crop. The first warehouse in the county was built in 1866 by L.C. Taylor. With the railroad arriving in town in 1881, business in Oxford really started to increase. In 1911, the Oxford Tobacco Research Station was established, and this facility has contributed a great deal to agricultural life in the country—for example the discovery of a wilt resistant tobacco plant.

Oxford became famous in the mid- to late 1800s for its educational institutions, being referred to as the "Athens of the South." Oxford Female College was formed in 1850, St. Johns College in 1857, the Oxford Orphanage in 1873, the Central Children's Home in 1883, Horner Military School in 1851 and Mary Potter School in 1890. Many people have contributed to the educational fabric of Oxford, such as John Chavis, C.G. Credle, J.F. Webb, Franklin Hobgood, James Horner, G.C. Shaw, Henry Cheatham, John Mills, Lizzie Hilliard and Nettie Bemis.

Culture has also been a strong contributor to the growth of Oxford. In 1888, the Opera House was opened, providing entertainment and education to citizens. Plays, musicals and lectures were held at the Opera House for many years. Many literary clubs have been, and continue to be, a part of Oxford's history—such as the Shakespeare Club, the Oxford Choral Society and the Tuesday Musical Club. The Oxford Woman's Club has been very instrumental in improving the culture of the town. Today the Granville County Historical Society Museum is very active in preserving our past.

The Long Company awaits your shopping in Oxford in 1925. *Photo courtesy of Granville County Historical Society Museum.*

Clarence Chambers and Wilbur Yeargin are in Yeargin's Warehouse in Oxford in 1970.
Photo courtesy of Jean Gill.

Oxford was advertised in the early 1900s as:

> [A]*n ideal seat of learning. The existence in it for well nigh a century of schools of high grade has developed culture and refinement in its citizens to an unusual degree. It is one of the prettiest towns in all the country, with wide and well-shaded streets paved and parked, granolithic walks, large lawns and elegant residences. It is one of the healthiest towns in the state. All the conditions of health—pure air, good water, mild but invigorating climate—are found here.*

Today Oxford remains a town that holds onto its past while still moving forward into the twenty-first century. It is a good place to call home, or just to visit. The Oxford of today still has the elegant old homes, wide shaded streets and many remembrances of its past. Most of all, it has good people. It is a town most of us will always remember fondly.

A Drive Through Oxford in 1886

Let's go back in time to 1886, and take a horse-and-buggy ride around Oxford with Mrs. L.E. Amis. Mrs. Amis wrote the following story for the *Oxford Torch Light* newspaper in 1886, which may be found in the Richard Thornton Library.

A Drive Through the City of Oxford

Come my friends, let us take a drive around this thrifty and beautiful town, and I will tell you about it as we go along. We will start here at the north end of College Street, how broad and pleasant it looks!

This classic name of this town is suggestive of mental culture, refinement and high art in every department and it is well worthy of its name. We are now passing by some pleasant looking residences, and on the left you see a handsome, spacious building of red brick—unique and tasteful in its structure, and surrounded by a magnificent grove of stately and umbrageous oaks. That is the "State Orphan Asylum" emanating first from the generous hearts of the Masons of North Carolina, and sustained by individual contribution, as well as by an appropriation from the State Legislature. It is under the control of trustees; but the present superintendent and manager, Dr. Dixon, is a well known and able minister, and a whole-souled, Christian gentleman, with a helpmeet who is an accomplished and true hearted woman, as well as a kind mother to the orphans. They have also a corps of excellent teachers, carefully and judiciously selected. The brick building in course of erection, beyond the Asylum hospital, is the Industrial School, where the orphans of both sexes will be taught how to earn a respectable living for themselves.

This new house with the mansard roof is to be the Episcopal Rectory and when it is finished will be both handsome and commodious.

We will turn down this new street now, and take a look at the "Granville Female Institute," a charge of Miss Bettie Clark, a most cultivated and thoroughly qualified principal; with a corps of accomplished assistants. Those numerous comfortable looking dwellings on the hill beyond, have all been erected by Mr. Richard Smith, an enterprising gentleman who has recently settled here, and his constant improvements are still going on.

We will now go around past the depot of the Oxford & Henderson Railroad, and view the handsome and commodious residence of Prof. J.H. Horner & Sons, co-principal of the "Horner Military School." The outbuildings are the academy and barracks, and it almost makes one wish to be a schoolboy, just to look at the spacious and tastefully ornamented grounds. We will now turn back, and driving past the steam gristmill owned by Mr. J.A. White, and all these great factories and warehouses we go around by the parsonage and the Presbyterian Church soon to be enlarged and renovated. I will say here, that there are nine resident ministers of the Gospel of Oxford, and the pulpits of each denomination are filled by most able and attractive divines.

We are now approaching another spacious and handsome structure, surrounded by extensive and richly ornamented grounds. This is "The Oxford Female Seminary." In charge of Prof. Hobgood, whose handsome genial face is enough in itself to make the school popular—and his corps of assistants is unsurpassed for highest culture and thorough competency. Here are many more handsome private residences, but we will now go past the Baptist Church and turn down Main Street, at the head of which stands among trees and flowers the beautiful home of A.H.A. Williams, Esq. On either side are many new and elegant private houses until we come to the busy center of the town. There stands the Oxford Bank Building, solid and imposing, erected and owned by Dr. Henry Herndon. Further on upon the same side but far back from the broad and pleasant street, stand among the trees and shrubbery this beautiful private residence.

And now we come to the rich and ever attractive display of stores. Let us stop before one of them. The name on the glass door is "A. Landis." He has two handsome sons with him in business and his clerks are all courteous and obliging gentlemen, (which is certainly characteristic of all the Oxford salesmen), and in this, as well as in the many other large stores, they are so numerous and so busy that one can almost imagine himself in one of the grand emporiums of New York. There across the street is the handsome hardware store of Messrs. Edwards and Rogers, and then come the handsome and richly furnished drugstores, which are always attractive, with the elegant and costly soda fountains, and the various wares that are so inviting to the eye as well as to the palate. We have already passed the

Methodist Church with its towering steeple and reaching the corner near Mr. Crawford's Drugstore, we will turn down into Commercial Avenue. Conspicuous up on the left is the elegant clothing store of the Kronheinmers, father and sons, and it is a first-class reliable house. At the further end of this broad street is the beautiful home of Oxford's dead. The cemetery is not large, but is tastefully laid out, and is well cared for by the ladies.

Now we will turn to the right, and soon we approach such an array of new and costly looking homes, on either side of the new "Broadway," that it looks as if we had come into the midst of another town. Nearly every one of these buildings and lots are owned by one citizen, the wealthy and enterprising Mr. B.H. Cozart. That palatial home in course of erection on the hill beyond is to be his personal residence, (and it is whispered that a lovely bride will soon be nestled there, but this is confidential).

The health of this beautiful thrifty young city, with its broad streets, its fine water, wholesome air and lovely shade trees, is unsurpassed. And now that there is no whiskey sold within its limits we have quiet, peaceful nights, and the attendance at the different churches has been greatly increased. The Young Men's Christian Association is a new and most desirable feature in its social element, and will doubtless be an active power for good to the entire city. The society of Oxford is refined, cultivated and delightful. The physicians are skillful and attentive when their services are needed and are a most genial and pleasant set of gentlemen, as are also the able and learned members of the legal profession. The boardinghouses are first-class, and are like pleasant homes to their patrons.

Now Ride with Me

Today I want to ask you to ride along with me as we spend a day in Oxford. Our goal is to soak in as much history as we can and to learn more about Granville County's past. I'll do the driving, so you just sit back and enjoy the sights and sounds of this historic county we call home.

Our first stop is Oxford City Hall, formerly Oxford High School and D.N. Hix School. Many old scenes from Oxford adorn the walls on both floors. Next we stop by the office of Al Woodlief, the mayor of Oxford. Mayor Woodlief really appreciates history and is knowledgeable about it, particularly Oxford. Upon entering his office, we get lucky, as Tom Ragland, former longtime city manager, is with Mayor Woodlief. Mr. Ragland is quite a local historian himself, so we spend a few minutes with these gentlemen.

Down the road we go, pulling onto the premises of the Granville County Historical Society Museum. We talk with Pam Thornton, the museum director, who shows us around the many exhibits, then takes us to the newly renovated old jail building that is loaded with historical information and artifacts from Granville County's bygone days. Pat Greene, one of the many museum guides, will greet you with a friendly smile and can answer your questions with her knowledge of local history. The gift shop in the museum has plenty of Granville County related items, such as books, postcards, T-shirts, Christmas ornaments and much more. On the way out of the museum we walk across Court Street to what is considered by many to be Oxford's landmark building, the Granville County Courthouse. This building has stood watch over downtown since its completion in 1840. Judge Dan Finch not only helps to administer justice in the county, but can enlighten us on many tidbits of local history. Judge Finch is a joy to talk with—so long as it is not when he is in his judicial robe with his gavel behind that huge bench and you are about to hear what your penalty is for your

Mary Bowling greets us in front of her store, Bowling's Store, on College Street in Oxford.

"mistake in judgment." The Granville County Courthouse was chosen by *Carolina Heritage* magazine in 2006 as one of the top ten historic courthouses in central North Carolina.

Exiting the courthouse onto Williamsboro Street, we cross over to the Granville County Sheriff's Department to see Deputy Sheriff Brin Wilkins. Brin has many pictures of former sheriffs and deputies, from patrolling the streets to busting old whiskey stills. As with many Granville Countians, Brin has an appreciation for history because he knows that "looking back" from time to time helps us move forward with more confidence in our steps. Brin can tell us all about law enforcement in the county and former sheriffs such as Roy Jones, Arthur Ray Currin and Marion Grissom. Present Sheriff David Smith also stops by for a chat, and he shares some of his many years of experience with us.

Down New College Street we go, stopping by the G.C. Shaw Museum. Mr. Shaw led the establishment of Mary Potter School, which opened in 1888. Here at the Shaw Museum we see old pictures and learn more about Oxford's history from Helen Amis. Mrs. Amis, a former librarian, is very knowledgeable about local history and is happy to share it. Now around the corner we go to the Oxford Police Station, where again we view pictures from Oxford's past, which hang along the walls. Police Chief John Wolford even includes old pictures of the department on the police department's website.

Next we drive over to College Street and admire some of the picturesque old homes that stand proudly as a testament to Oxford's past and future. C.G. Credle School, built in 1911, still educates young people who will someday be leaders in their town. We now drive through the campus of the Masonic Home for Children, which became the first orphanage in North Carolina when it opened in 1873, and to this day is a home for children. To get a real sense of this place, we stop by the Archives Department, and see artifacts, pictures, books and other relics of a bygone era. Pat Colenda simply does a wonderful job of preserving this great institution's past as the historian-archivist here. We next stop by the Central Children's Home, which also serves a vital function and today, as it has since 1887, continues to be a big part of Oxford's history. We walk through Cheatham Hall, on the National Register of Historic Places, named for Henry Cheatham, longtime superintendent and former United States congressman.

You never know what you might find at our next stop, Harry's Trash and Treasures. Harry Jones is the proprietor here, and his antique store is simply loaded with old things. Harry is quite a friendly fellow and knows a bit of history also. You really step into the past upon entering this place. Across the street from Harry's is Elmwood Cemetery, and we drive slowly through its meandering roads and read tombstone inscriptions from many of Granville's past citizens. The Horners, Hunts, Thomases, Lyons, Hays, Miltons, Coopers, Hobgoods and other names rest atop the serene gravesites shaded by stately trees. Elmwood is truly a lovely place, with its narrow roads curving through its well-cared for grounds, bearing testament to former county citizens. I know driving through cemeteries might be seen by some as a weird habit, and my good wife, Beth, reminds me of this, but I really enjoy driving slowing through cemeteries, enjoying the peace and reading the epitaphs on the tombstones. Closer to downtown, we walk through the Old Oxford Cemetery. Across the street we stop by Granville Barbershop to see Harold Slaughter, who has cut many a head of hair in town, and who can probably compare your hair to your father's or your grandfather's. Harold's Barbershop is a popular place in downtown Oxford, where you can not only get your hair neatly trimmed in an old-style barber chair, but also enjoy some good conversation with local people.

Before I wear you out, we will stop by Jones Drugstore for lunch. This author remembers ordering many a vanilla milkshake and grilled cheese sandwich at the old lunch counter as a young boy, while "helping out," (or "getting in the way"), at my mother's (Mary Bowling) store on College Street. Upon leaving Jones Drugstore, we bump into local historian Eddie McCoy, who is a very friendly man. After lunch, we walk over to Haskin's Realty, and step into Joe Haskins office. Here we learn about Harvey Bullock, an Oxford native who wrote many of the scripts for *The Andy Griffith Show*. Andy, Barney, Opie, Aunt Bee and others seem to come alive in Joe's great collection of show memorabilia. Just down the street, we walk into the Granville County Chamber of Commerce office, where Ginnie Currin greets us with her usual warm smile, and gives us facts and figures on the growth of both Oxford and the county.

Episcopal Bookstore is our next destination. There we can find items related to and about Granville County, and owner Harrison Simons is an excellent source of information for local history. Our last destination for today is the Richard Thornton Library. Oxford's downtown library is an excellent resource to learn about our past, from looking at old newspapers and books, to reading the Hayes Collection and folders of information on subjects related to county history. If there is anything we need, Fann Montague of the library staff will help us. Fann is very knowledgeable about methods of historical research.

I hope you have enjoyed riding along with me through this place some of us proudly call home—Oxford.

A Visit to Oxford in 1908

The following story is from the *Durham Sun* in 1908, written by one of its reporters after a visit to Oxford:

Oxford is a beautiful town. Its stately oaks and wide, shaded streets breathe the air of dignified age and calm repose. Oxford is full of historic reminiscences and pleasing memories. Oxford has handsome residences dotting heretofore vacant lots, and two railroads. The town is different from what it was thirty years ago, where only the bright golden leafed tobacco made the denizens rich and when she sat in quietude, amid her educational and literary prestige.

Our visit over there yesterday was fraught with much pleasure. Old friends remembered us, and to J.F. Edwards, a prosperous hardware dealer, and Mr. R.W. Lassiter, the popular banker, are we indebted for contributions to the chimes fund. May the bells of joy always gladly ring in their hearts.

A splendid dinner was served at the Exchange Hotel, run by L.F. Smith. A visit to the Oxford Orphan Asylum is a revelation and inspiration. We have seen the work in its infancy, when Jack Mills was putting his life and soul into the work, and it is now an enlarged edition of his work carried on by the Masons. There are now under the care of this institution 320 boys and girls. It will do your heart good to see them. A delightful entertainment was given in the chapel that was witnessed by a packed house. General B.S. Royster, in his usual ornate style, delivered a charming address of the highest human emotions and words of earnestness. The work at the asylum of Superintendent Hicks, and guarding spirit of the children, Miss Bemis, is one the people cannot be too well acquainted with.

An early 1900s Oxford firetruck.

No one could see the lovely homes here, so stately and so in keeping with colonial architecture, the wide streets and magnificent trees without breaking the commandment, "Thou shalt not covet thy neighbor's home." Mr. Littlejohn, who laid off this town, had rare visions for his day.

The following were businesses located on Hillsboro Street in Oxford in 1942: Basement Barber Shop, Oxford National Bank, Pender's Store, Turner's Market, Ira Evans Shoe Repair, A&P Food Store, Leggetts Department Store, Avery's Store, Busy Bee Café, Horner Brothers Company, Morton Hardware, Oxford Hardware, Barsel's Café, Granville Feed Store, Imperial Billiard Parlor, Bergen's General Merchandise, Farmer's Café, Buchanon's Grocery, Montague Brothers, Blalock Chevrolet, Western Auto, Banner Warehouse, Hotel Oxford, Hotel Oxford Coffee Shop, Hotel Smoke Shop, Palace Café, Talley's Furniture, Magnum Warehouse, Old Cemetery, Owen Motor Company, Ideal Service Station, Carrington Supply, B+N Motor Company, No. 2 Planter's Warehouse, Harlem Barber Shop and Ray Lumber Company.

Among the businesses on College Street were: William's Drug, Oxford Furniture, Union National Bank, Carolina Telephone, Breedlove Grocery, Ideal Fruit and Grocery, Lyon Drugstore, Johnson Warehouse, City Meet Market, Baird Hardware, Owen Warehouse and No. 1 Chapman Lumber.

In 1877, this was written about Granville County in *Branson's North Carolina Business Directory*:

Granville has pleasantly undulating land, well watered by the head branches of the Tar River—soil generally remunerative. This is altogether a fine county, and contains a thrifty population of 24,831, white 11,467, colored 13,355. Tobacco is the great staple. The weed is produced to perfection, and manufactured largely. Wheat, corn, oats, sweet potatoes are grown extensively and profitably.

Christmas Celebrations

Let's look back on how Oxford and Granville County celebrated Christmases past. Most of the following reports are from old *Oxford Public Ledgers* and the Francis Hays Collection in the Richard Thornton Library.

December 20, 1924
Tonight at the Courthouse, the "Old Temple of Justice" will be performed by the Oxford Boys Convert Band. The manly little musicians will rend the air with Christmas music using their new musical instruments, as their gift to the people of Oxford.

December 20, 1935
The Christmas Opening Night found throngs of people in Oxford for the entertainment at the courthouse and for a visit to the stores. Badger Chandler's String Band, with Badger doing the dance numbers and Red Cox assisting, the string band from the CCC, Tobie's Band and Tom Elkerson's dance brought down the house with applause. Ed Coble, who presided over the program with Miss Beth Watkins, was master of the occasion, bringing out frequent bits of spontaneous wit. Businessmen reported a large number of shoppers in their stores and buying was generous.

December 25, 1904
Theodore Kingsburg wrote the following in 1904 about his remembrances of celebrating Christmas in Oxford:

> *The boys on Christmas Eve made much noise with their Chinese crackers, and bells were rung. Quite early on Christmas morning, the church bells and the Courthouse bell rang out their music on the cold air, and at this*

The South Granville Band marches down Main Street in Oxford in a Christmas Parade. *Courtesy of Granville County Historical Society Museum.*

Oxford's inhabitants were quickly aroused. Early in the morning the flowing bowls of eggnog were prepared in most of the homes. On Christmas night there was usually a dancing party given at the local hotel. If, as was often the case, the several large millponds were covered with ice, a part of the day was certain to be spent in skating, and nearly all the men and boys were experts, and some of the females also. Many would ride in carriages to witness the skating and applaud the skill of brothers or sweethearts. Many of the old men were capital skaters, and also "took a hand." If perchance Christmas was snowy, the sleighs pulled by horses would be filled with young and old properly robed for the occasion. If Christmas night was one of moonshine the sleighs would be more numerous, and doubtless words of love were whispered as the fine horses sped along the decorated streets of Oxford.

December 23, 1941

Approximately 4,500 people thronged downtown Oxford Friday night for the Formal Christmas Opening. "The weather was just about perfect, Santa Claus was in fine fettle, the stores were beautifully decorated and everyone had a good time," said W.T. Yancey, president of the Merchants Association. The parade moved down Main Street to the post office, where it circled back to a spot in front of the county courthouse and Santa gave out gifts of candy and toys. Downtown stores remained open until 9 o'clock and merchants reported that business was brisk.

December 30, 1949

Children and oldsters have appeared all over town displaying evidence of a visit from Santa Claus. Chief of Police J.L. Cash increased the night patrol prior to Christmas and no break-ins have occurred. College boys and girls, home for the holidays, have kept the social wheel in a merry spin with parties, drugstore confabs and tavern dancing.

December 14, 1951

The arrival of Santa was preceded by a truckload of carolers, which rolled into Main Street. The singers were under the direction of Virgil Alexander of the Oxford High School Music Department. Shortly thereafter, the lively-stepping high school band tumbled up Main, with their scantily clad girls, marching to the notes of "Here Comes Santa Claus." The crowd was estimated at four thousand.

Street Names

If you are at all like me, street names are hard to remember. I feel like I can get to any place in Oxford or Granville County, but just don't ask me to give you the name of the street or road I used to get there. Someone recently asked me how to get to Harry's Trash and Treasures and it took me ten minutes to come up with Harris Street, even though I have stopped there many times.

Street names in Oxford usually have a historical significance. Coggeshall Street was named for Dr. George Coggeshall, who owned property in the area. College Street was originally Grassy Creek Street, and Court Street is thus named for its proximity to the Granville County Courthouse. Hillsboro Street was once called the Tar River Street, and Kingsbury Street was named after Dr. Theodore Kingsbury, a newspaper editor. Littlejohn Street

Above: A little snow has visited Oxford's Main Street. *Photo courtesy of Granville County Historical Society Museum.*

Opposite: You are now riding down Hillsboro Street in Oxford around 1940. *Photo courtesy of Granville County Historical Society Museum.*

is named in honor of Thomas Littlejohn, who sold the land on which the town of Oxford was built. McClanahan Street honors General William Smith McClanahan, and Military Street runs alongside where Horner Military School once stood. Standard Street was named after the Standard Oil Company, which once did a booming business in Oxford.

Hall's Drugstore

Hall's Drugstore was once a focal point of Oxford. Its Main Street location was a favorite shopping spot, and a place to gather for a cold fountain drink and to catch up on the latest town news. John Perry Hall, whose father John G. Hall started Hall's Drugstore in 1879, wrote the following about growing up and working in the drugstore:

> Father said before there was an ice plant in Oxford, he would take some men to Ridley's pond on the old Henderson Road and cut ice off the pond and pack it in sawdust in the basement of Hall's and use it during the year for making ice cream. In the early days, Hall's had two soda fountains, one on one side for whites and the other for blacks. One of the most exciting times of the year for me as a child of eight to ten came at Christmas. Then Sam and I sold fireworks at Hall's. There were no restrictions on the sale or firing of these firecrackers, roman candles, baby wakers, torpedoes, etc. A certain section of the store was marked off and no smoking was allowed there. A big bonfire was built in the middle of the street. Every now and then a "big spender" would come in and buy a 12-inch baby waker, which cost all of a dollar, and throw this in the street fire. When this went off sparks were thrown high in the air. Several of us boys looked forward to going with Mr. Arch Taylor and his boys early every Christmas morning all over town shooting fireworks. We would set our clocks for 3:00 a.m. and stay until breakfast time. I can remember how Hall's used to look around Christmastime in those days, with horns and drums and toys strung overhead across the store and lots of fruit, nuts and candy displayed.
>
> Another really big day in Oxford in those years was St. John's Day, the 24th of June, commemorating the St. John's School, which later became the Oxford Masonic Orphanage. The railroads ran excursions into

Hall's Drugstore is to the right of the Carolina Theater in Oxford in the 1950s.

Oxford. The Seaboard Station was being Hall's Drugstore on the corner of Gilliam and Littlejohn Street. These crowds came by Hall's and Sam and I had a lemonade and ice cream stand on the Main Street in front of the store. All along College Street heading to the orphanage there were similar lemonade stands.

In those days Hall's was a gathering place for men after supper to tell tales, smoke, chew and whittle around the big, warm pot-bellied stove we had in the center of the store to heat the building. There were no TVs or radios, but we were open until 10 o'clock. So after supper men would come in and take the chairs placed around the store. Before long some man would say, "a dollar is a man's friend," and that would start an argument. Men I can remember being present a lot of nights were Dr. E.T. White, J.K. Blackwell, Charlie Garmen, Dr. Cannady (my uncle), Col. Rome Horner, Zeb Patterson, Dr. Sam Watkins, Dr. Nat Daniel, Dr. Thomas and lots of others. Father's desk was nearby, as was Uncle Gus's and from time to time they would get up and put in their two cents worth.

During those years there were several rooms over the store, occupied by doctors' offices, study rooms, Upham's Electuary and men who came from the country and worked in Hall's.

Along in 1932 and 1933 came the Depression. Business came to a standstill. There was very little money. Hall's took in around $40.00 a day. On Saturday, the big day of the week, if we got up to $200.00 we had a big day. Prescriptions were generally fifty cents to $1.00 each. We sold peanuts for ten cents a pound. Our salaries were low—generally

Ray Lumber Company had an entrant in the Hoover Cart Parade. The parade was in "recognition" of President Herbert Hoover, and was held during the Depression.

$40.00 per month. My pharmacist salary was reduced to $75.00 per month. We lived off our "fat." We, as other merchants, extended credit to our good customers. No one had much cash. We were all in the same boat.

I think it was during this time that "Hoover Carts" were popular. These "carts" (so called) named after President Hoover, who was blamed for the Depression, had an auto axle and two wheels and tires with a makeshift seat on top, pulled by a mule or horse. People had no money to buy gas for a car.

Before 1934 Hall's had practically all male clerks. Miss Virginia Carr kept books at the store and was one of the first ladies we had. At nights she played piano at Orpheum Theatre. Then came Miss Addie Breedlove, and then, when she married Earl Hunt, she left Hall's and Miss Norma Breedlove came to work at Hall's. I cannot find the words to tell how much she has meant to Hall's Drugstore. Every inch a lady, and a super salesperson. Miss Norma was the only lady in the drugstore for a long time. Many ladies have helped since, however, including Margaret Saunders, Lois Vaughan, Mary Smith, Rachel Brummitt, Gertrude Daniel, Jennie Wilson, Gladys Montague, Brenda Parham, Hattie Smith and Ann Brooks.

Happenings around Stovall

Back in the early to mid-1900s, two amazing sites were located near Stovall. According to *National Geographic* magazine, the largest holly tree in the world was located about a mile from Stovall. This tree was estimated to be one hundred feet in height, as measured by the *National Geographic* photographers who visited in the 1930s. This huge holly tree gave evidence of nature's splendor, but fifty yards away stood a testament to the craftsmanship of man.

Here stood what was believed in the 1930s to be the second largest house in North Carolina, next to the Biltmore House in Asheville. The old Dickerson House had forty-eight rooms. E.N. Dickerson, a New York lawyer, was the owner who enlarged the house gradually over time. Poor health had brought Dickerson to Stovall. He enjoyed the climate and the hunting lands in the area, and also the world famous Buckhorn Mineral Springs in nearby Bullock. Dickerson accumulated wealth through his proactive work as a patent attorney, appearing in two famous cases: Bell Telephone and McCormick Reaper. In fact, Alexander Graham Bell, inventor of the telephone, visited Dickerson in Stovall.

Dickerson only lived in Stovall for portions of the year, using it mostly as a vacation spot. But he made his mark in the area, paying taxes on land he did not own just for hunting privileges, building his own ice plant and paying for a building in Stovall that had a drugstore, opera hall and other retail businesses.

After Dickerson sold the house, W.C. Daniel helped him move. Mr. Daniel came across a letter inquiring about the whereabouts of "Andrew Jackson's head," and wanting to know if Dickerson still had the head. Mr. Daniel immediately knew what the letter was about. In 1834, Samuel Dewey, who hated Jackson, sawed the wood figurehead off the bow of the

The Gregory Mill in Stovall. *Photo courtesy of Herbert Gregory Jr.*

ship *Old Ironsides*. Dewey then gave the sawed-off wooden head of Jackson to Dickerson's grandfather, who passed it to his grandson, who, in turn, kept it in the Dickerson place in Stovall. Mr. Daniel had seen the head on numerous occasions, and had helped ship it up north after Dickerson moved. This wooden head eventually ended up in the Naval Academy. Amazingly, President Franklin Roosevelt wrote a letter to Mr. Daniel in Stovall, thanking him for his help.

Of course Stovall, formerly called Sassafras Fork, can be proud of many other historical achievements. One of the signers of the Declaration of Independence, John Penn, lived near Stovall. The Gregory brothers, William and Francis, introduced flue-cured tobacco to Canada. Also, one of North Carolina's first scoutmasters, Luther Wilkerson, had his Boy Scout troop in Stovall chartered in 1911.

A Letter of Encouragement

The following letter was written by J.S. Hardaway, a former pastor of Oxford Baptist Church. It is addressed to Margaret Currin of Oxford, who later in life married Robert Lassiter, a wealthy road builder and civic leader of Granville County. The letter dates from 1904, when Mr. Hardaway wrote a condolence letter to Margaret, one of his church members, on the death of her sister, Eva.

All of us have, or will, experience the loss of someone we love. Perhaps this letter, so full of comforting words, can help ease the burden when death comes to someone you know and love. The letter was saved by Virginia Currin Thompson of Goldsboro, a relative of Margaret Currin. Two years later, Eva would be dead.

My dear Sister Currin,

I wish I could go into your home today and carry in person the deep and tender sympathy I feel for you. Human sympathy is sweet, but it is so weak. It cannot do anything for us, but assures us of a fellow feeling for us in our grief. But there is one, our dear Savior, who can be touched with a feeling of our infirmities, who can bear our sorrow if we let him. I hope your sorrow is even now soothed by his loving sympathy, and that you can hear him gently saying, "Come unto me all ye that labor and are heavy laden, and I will give you rest." Our Father in his love sends these trials upon us, "Who the Lord loveth, He chasteneth." But while passages from God's word abound, to assure us that afflictions come from God's loving hand, sometimes we are dazed by them, and stagger under them.

Longfellow, the poet, wrote, "Afflictions not from the ground arise, but oftentimes celestial benedictions assume this dark disguise." Let us look at our sorrow a little while, Eva is dead. Is that true? No, that is

Virginia Carroll waters the flowers in front of her store, Virginia's Gift Shop, in Oxford. *Photo courtesy of Virginia Carroll.*

not true. "She is not dead, the child of our affection, but gone into that school where she no longer needs our protection and Christ himself doth rule." She had just laid aside the sufferings and the burdens of this mortal state and entered upon the glories and joys of the life immortal. "For if we believe that Jesus died and rose again, even so them also that are fallen asleep in Jesus will God bring with him."

I cannot tell you fully the estimate I set upon her. In physical beauty she was well nigh perfect. Lovely in form and feature, there was absolutely nothing in the way of blemish about her. Her manners were sweet and winsome. As a church member, she grew more beautiful year by year. Large hearted, sympathetic, generous, charitable, hospitable—she was entering upon a life of wide influence. It seems like an irreparable loss, her early death. It would be nothing short of a terrible disaster but for the fact that God rules.

There are doubtless many lessons our Heavenly Father is teaching you all through this great bereavement. One is this: the only thing that is worth setting our hearts upon is heaven. There only can we find perfect joy and peace. "These are the good and blest, those we love most and best, there too we soon shall rest, heaven is our home."

Dear friend, I assure you from my heart that I am distressed at Eva's death. For Brother Currin and yourself, for Lonie, Nellie, and Maggie, for Eugene and Willy, and for that little motherless girl.

May God comfort you all.

J.H. Hardaway.

Ed Meadows, All-American

He was an All-American football player at Duke University and a guest on *The Ed Sullivan Show*. He played for six years in the NFL and was voted Most Valuable Player on the 1955 Pittsburgh Steelers team. He made one of the most famous tackles in NFL history on All Pro quarterback Bobby Layne of the Detroit Lions.

This outstanding athletic career belongs to one of Oxford's own, Ed Meadows. Born in 1932 to parents Edward and Aileen Meadows, Ed graduated from Oxford High School (present-day City Hall) in 1950. Ed was simply a terror on the football field for OHS. During his senior year, OHS outscored its opponents 256 to 46, including Erwin (40 to 6) and Durham County (26 to 0). The team was coached by R.C. Culton.

Meadows was quite the BMOC (Big Man On Campus) while at Oxford High School. According to *The Owl*, the school paper, Meadows was well liked by the ladies for his good looks, and admired by the men for his athletic prowess. Young Ed was affectionately called "Tarzan" around campus for his muscular build and size. Ed would eventually play for the NFL at six feet three inches tall and 225 pounds. He would be considered big among men today, but in the 1950s he was huge for a man. *The Owl* also recorded that young Ed liked to jitterbug and his favorite song was "Bowlegged Woman."

After high school, Ed was recruited by Duke Coach Bill Murray to play for the Blue Devils. As mentioned earlier, Meadows became an All-American and now is enshrined as one of the greatest players in Duke football history. Defensive tackle was his position.

Ed, nicknamed "Country Meadows," had perhaps his best collegiate performance in a game against North Carolina in 1952, which Duke won 34 to 0. Meadows had fifteen tackles in the game according to Tarheel Head

Ed Meadows while a student athlete at Duke University. *Photo courtesy of Brent Meadows.*

Coach Carl Snavely after the game. "Meadows is the finest tackle I've seen in a long time, and is also as mean a tackle that has lined up against us. In football, of course, mean is good." An Army coach after a game against Duke said this: "Meadows is a real standout. This boy covers all of the field; he can run like a deer. He rushes the passer, blocks kicks and makes tackles from one end of the line to the other. He really roams, and once he gets to you he will lay a wallop on you."

Oxford was really proud of Ed as his national fame grew while at Duke. Before a game at Army in New York, the following telegram was sent:

To Coach Bill Murray—From the hometown of Ed Meadows, Oxford, NC—Best wishes for success against Army—From Mr. and Mrs. George Duffy, Mr. and Mrs. John Myers, Mr. and Mrs. Tom Johnson, Nancy Watkins, Grady Harris, Elizabeth Floyd, Charlotte Crews, Vivian Davis, Boothe Crews, Thad Stem, Nellie McFarland, Mrs. T.G. Stem Sr., Nat Burwell, Rev. and Mrs. R.N. White, Mr. and Mrs. Frank Bullock, Dr. and Mrs. James Bradsher, Mr. and Mrs. O.P. Sutherland, Naomi Boring, Mr. and Mrs. David Hix.

In 1954 Meadows was drafted by the Chicago Bears, coached by the legendary George Halas. Meadows had an outstanding career in the National Football League, but he is especially remembered for a vicious hit on Detroit Lions quarterback Bobby Lane. The tackle lifted Layne completely off his feet and caused a concussion. The Lions claimed it was a dirty play—that Meadows had hit Layne after Layne had pitched the ball. This hit was the talk of sports news around the country, spotlighting the violence of the game. Here is how a sportswriter in Chicago summed up what happened in the game at Wrigley Field:

Layne pitched the ball to a running back, then turned to watch the play. Suddenly, the lights went out. What happened was the 225 pounds of Chicago Bears defensive lineman, all of it named Ed Meadows, had blindsided Bobby with enough force to level any reasonably well-constructed brick building. Bobby was down and out for the count. They carried him off the field for the day with a concussion.

Ironically, Meadows, who played with a fire in his eyes, was later thrown out of the game for punching another player while Layne was at a local hospital.

Along with being a feared player in the NFL, Meadows was a busy family man. He married Patricia Kennelly of Texas and had four children—Patricia, Beverly, Edward and Mary. After his playing days were over, Meadows moved to Raleigh and bought a couple of tire stores. Tragically, Meadows died at the young age of forty-two in 1974. He is buried in his hometown of Oxford, where he began a career that perhaps is unparalleled in Granville County history.

Some "Goings On" in 1914

James Daniel of Butner sent me a few *Granville Enterprise* newspapers from 1914. I found the following excerpts rather interesting. Maybe you will also.

THE STAFF OF LIFE

I have it—nothing equal to it. Just bought five hundred bushels of selected white country corn, which I am having ground into meal at the best watermill in the county. If you want something good, try it. Remember too, that as we should not live by bread alone, I have all the other seasonable goods, such as country bacon, lye homing, green black-eyed peas, lima beans, dried apples, evaporated peaches, hominy grits and everything the very best. Phone me quick, phone 52.

—L. Thomas

THINGS "A DOING" ROUND TOWN

Mrs. W.Z. Mitchell has been suffering from a rising on her ear, and went to Durham for treatment. She is much better.

We understand that the Orpheum Theater has several good plays booked for early dates.

Mr. I.T. Hobgood lost a fine horse last week.

OAK HILL ITEMS

If we take the trouble to find the cause of the increase in crimes among our people, we will find that most of it is attributable to strong drink. Thirty or forty years ago men drank whiskey, but it did not make them vicious as it

Crystal Hill in the Bullock Community.

now does. It ruins the body and mind. Why a man will take the bread from his wife and children and put it in whiskey is too hard for me.

The St. Johns Day celebration at the Oxford Orphanage is well nigh on us. The railroads are arranging special schedules, speakers are getting in shape and the pigs are ready to become "roast pig." And next to "roast pig" as its chief feature, the celebration is famous as the one time of the year when the Granville girl and her life from Vance, Wake, Durham and Person appear at their best, pleasing to the eye of the old and a feast to that of the young man. Of minor interest is the fact that Mr. D.G. Brummit will deliver an address, but to the crowd as a whole this is a feature of minor importance, for it wants "roast pig," lemonade and a look at a real good-looking girl.

EDITORIAL

A lack of knowledge of the value of money on the part of women is the most powerful enemy to domestic happiness that exists. We are proud of the American woman, her intelligence, her charm and her achievement, but it must be admitted that in too many instances she is far from a careful saver or a wise spender. It is not entirely a love of ease and luxury that lays our women open to the charge of extravagance, although that is an important factor in the case. Perhaps a more frequent cause is inefficiency in the business side of housekeeping.

Education

Education is a better safeguard of liberty than a standing army.
                                        —*Edward Everett*

To say that education has changed over the years is quite an understatement. Did the old days produce a better learning environment for students in Granville County than today? The old days: back when the three R's were stressed; back when, if you misbehaved, a clear message was sent to your head through a whack to your backside; back when what you did throughout the year counted more than an end of year test; back when manners and respect for others were as important as math. Or do today's students enjoy a better learning environment? In Granville County, our young people now have access to instant information through computers and television, students of different races attend school together, going to college is now more accessible and school facilities are very good. Other comparisons can be made. For example, it used to be that one failed his grade if he did not do satisfactory work, a policy which opposes today's "social promotion" theory in which it seems students are sometimes passed to the next grade regardless of their academic record so as not to "hurt their feelings."

For what it's worth, I tend to think that today's students are better off. We have a fine school system here in our county. However, it is important to hold onto those educational traditions from our past that were, and

Opposite top: C.G. Credle Elementary School students in the library in 1967.
Opposite middle:Grove Hill School in the early 1900s.
Opposite bottom:A Granville County school bus is ready to take these students to school. *Photo courtesy Granville County Historical Society Museum.*

No. 88-A

THIS body is 88 inches wide by 13 feet in length (not including the cowl) and seats 40 to 50. Especially recommended for any chassis of 130" wheelbase. Built the Sturdy *Oxford* way of steel and oak and beautifully finished in green, striped in yellow. This body is also furnished in 17 foot and 19 foot lengths (not including cowl) for chassis 175" and 200".

Back of every *Oxford* "Iron Bound" Bus Body is 40 years of experience in building good vehicle bodies. *Oxford* bodies were the first school bus bodies built in the South . . . and they remain first in beauty, strength, comfort, safety and economy.

OXFORD BODY COMPANY, OXFORD, N. C.
FORTY YEARS EXPERIENCE

An advertisement for the Oxford Body Company, which built school buses.

continue to be, so valuable—learn from history to better navigate the present and future.

Without question, many things have changed for the better. Back in the early 1900s, most of Granville County's schools were taught by one teacher. These small, rural schools were spread through the county. There were schools in Hester, Knap of Reeds, Parham, Willow Branch, Culbreth, Enon, Salem, Royster, Northside, Sharon, Providence, Tally Ho, Tar River, Cornwall, Bethel, Penny Hill, Dexter, Grassy Creek, Gray Rock, Satterwhite and many other places. Most of these facilities were poorly equipped and one teacher taught all of the grades.

Mr. John Frederick Webb led the push for consolidation of county schools. Webb was Granville County Schools' superintendent from 1907 to 1935. J.F. Webb High School is named in his honor. Mr. Webb's son, James, later served as head of our nation's space agency, NASA, in the 1960s, and was most instrumental in our landing on the moon in 1969. What an honor it is for us to have an Oxford native play such a prominent role in this historic event!

One aspect of our past that needs to be brought back into school, I think most of us will agree, is discipline and respect. Of course, these characteristics are best taught at home. The following is from Oxford's Horner Military School's guidelines of 1891:

The discipline is not severe, but firm and decided, and boys who are not willing to make up their minds to comply cheerfully with the regulations of the school are urged not to apply for admission. Boys whose influence is felt to be injurious to the morals and scholarship of their fellows will be removed from the school.

Opposite top: The 1919 Mary Potter School baseball team. *Photo courtesy of G.C. Shaw Museum.*
Opposite middle: A Granville County school class taking a break from their studies.
Opposite bottom: Mabel Harris with her first-grade class at Stem School in 1933. *Photo courtesy of Mabel Harris.*

Dr. Dorothy Pruitt's home economics class visiting the Peggy Mann TV show in Durham. Pictured from left to right are Peggy Mann, Hazel Long, Betty Howard, Flora Watkins, Sandra Day, Betty DeMent, Carolyn Jones, Patricia Woodlief, Betsy Howard, Susan Daniel, Wilbra Shearin, Ginger Burwell and Nancy Farabow. *Photo courtesy of the Granville County Historical Society Museum.*

Another good attribute from Horner Military School from this time was the daily requirement of thirty minutes of exercise, which was then called physical culture. Healthy students tend to perform better academically. As Rousseau said:

> *Do you, then, want to cultivate your pupil's intelligence? Exercise his body continually; make him robust and healthy in order to make him wise and reasonable, Let him work, be active, run, yell, always be in motion. Let him be a man in his vigor, and soon he will be one in his reason.*

Oxford's Orphanages

To provide family centered services via an appropriate period of residential group care for children and youth from ages 4–21, who cannot remain at home due to dependency, neglect or abuse, by providing a wholesome atmosphere that is conducive to their emotional, educational, social, spiritual and physical growth and development, which promotes positive family functioning and/or independent living.
—Mission Statement of the Central Children's Home

The Central Children's Home has been a proud part of Oxford's history since its founding in 1887. Under its current director, Michael Alston, this fine institution continues to grow and expand its services. The campus is very pretty, especially the Cheatham Dining Hall and Auditorium, and is on the National Register of Historical Places. The dining hall and auditorium are named for Henry Cheatham, who served as the superintendent of the orphanage for twenty-eight years. Cheatham had earlier served as the only African American member of the United States House of Representatives from 1889 to 1893.

Augustus Shepard is the founder of the Central Children's Home. Augustus Shepard was the father of James Shepard, the founder of North Carolina Central University in Durham. This institution was first called "The Grant Colored Asylum of North Carolina" in honor of President Ulysses Grant. Upon its incorporation in 1887, through the visionary leadership and hard work of both Shepard and Cheatham, what is now called the Central Children's Home became the second orphanage to be founded in North Carolina, and one of the very first to serve black children in the country.

There were hard times in the early years, just as problems exist today for any institution providing such essential services to those in need. In 1893,

The Oxford Colored Orphanage Band. This orphanage is now known as the Central Children's Home. *Photo courtesy of Mike Alston.*

Cheatham Hall is located on the campus of the Central Children's Home in Oxford. *Photo courtesy of the Granville County Historical Society Museum.*

the children received no Christmas presents except for one small piece of stick candy donated by the missionary society of Kittrell. There was always the matter of how many funds would be allocated to the home by the legislature. Much credit goes to the Duke brothers of Durham, who became wealthy from Bull Durham Tobacco. Benjamin Duke donated the money for the Angier B. Duke School on the Central Children's Home campus. In 1924, under the will of James B. Duke, the Duke Endowment made provisions to aid the orphanage. There has also been a cordial relationship through the years between the Masonic Home for Children and the Central Children's Home, which have both played such an important role in shaping Oxford's history. In 1929, the Masonic Home donated 102 beds and 250 chairs to the Central Children's Home. In 1942, the children of the Central Home visited the Masonic Home and gave them fruits and vegetables from their farm.

Other people gave their time and support to the orphanage, such as Ben Lassiter, Frank Hancock, Benjamin Parham, Francis Gregory and Dr. W.N. Thomas. Dr. Thomas served as the home's physician for thirty years, most of the time donating his services simply because the children needed medical care. In fact, for many years, Dr. Thomas and his wife, Estelle, personally bought and delivered Christmas presents for sometimes over two hundred children.

Many people have served the home over the years, too many to mention them all here. Notable among those who served are: Lena Smith, who served as teacher and principal for thirty-four years; Jauncey McDougle, who was budget officer for fifty years; Joseph Dixon, who taught the children brick making for close to fifty years; and Joseph Goodloe, who served as chairman of the board for twenty-three years.

Granville County
and the Civil War

Granville County played a major role in the Civil War, with over fifteen hundred men participating in the conflict. Among the units called into action, the most well known was the Granville Grays, captained by George Wortham. Other units were the Granville Ploughboys, the Granville Stars and the Granville Rifles. A camp was built along Providence Road for soldiers to train before going off to war.

There were no battles fought in Granville County, but the War Between the States greatly affected the people of the county. By 1861, when the Civil War started, there were over ten thousand slaves in Granville County. The war also stopped plans to build two academies, Tally Ho Female Academy and Oak Hill Military Academy, in Granville County. On February 18, 1861, the North Carolina General Assembly passed the following resolution:

> *Section 1. Be it enacted by the General Assembly of the State of North Carolina, and it is hereby enacted by the authority of the same, That John L. Jones, Samuel D. Ferrill, John W. Booth, John Flemings and James A. Russel, their associates and successors, be, and they are hereby declared a body politic and corporate, to be known and designated by the name of the "Trustees of Tally Ho Female Academy," situated at Tally Ho, in the county of Granville, and by that name shall have perpetual succession, and shall acquire, receive and hold such moneys, chattels and lands as may be necessary to accomplish the purposes of the institution.*

Then on February 22, 1861, the General Assembly passed another act to build Oak Hill Military Academy:

Section 1. Be it enacted by the General Assembly of North Carolina, and it is hereby enacted by the authority of the same, That W.G. Thomas, M.T. Smith, B.P. Tharp, Richard Tharp and Peterson Tharp, and their successors, be, and they are hereby incorporated and made a body politic, under the name and style of the "Trustees of Oak Hill Military Academy," in the county of Granville, with the usual right, powers, privileges and duties of such corporations.

Lieutenant Colonel Tazewell Hargrove from Granville achieved notoriety during the Civil War. On June 26, 1863, at the South Anna Bridge in Virginia, Hargrove led his troops, numbering eighty, in holding off an attack of over fifteen hundred Yankees for more than four hours. Armed only with rifles against the enemies' vast number of men and their two cannons, Hargrove's men were finally overrun and many of the eighty were killed. The Yankees suffered many casualties also. Hargrove and a few of his men were captured and imprisoned. Colonel Spear, who led the Union troops, stated later that "The resistance made by the Confederates was the most stubborn I had known during the war, I supposed that we were fighting four hundred infantry instead of eighty." After the war, Hargrove was awarded the Confederate Medal of Honor, one of only forty-eight soldiers to receive the award. He served as attorney general of North Carolina from 1873 to 1877.

Another Granville County man to gain fame during the Civil War was Benjamin Person Thorp. Thorp served with the North Carolina Fifty-fifth Regiment while they were at Gettysburg in July 1863. Thorp was known as a sharpshooter, and was ordered by his lieutenant to shoot at an enemy soldier who was on his horse surveying the battlefield. The problem was that his soldier was more than seven hundred yards away. Thorp fired and missed, then climbed twelve feet up a cherry tree and hit his target. The soldier Thorp killed turned out to be one of the Union's most respected men, General John F. Reynolds.

Following is a letter written by John Harris of Granville County to his sister Bettie. It shows vividly the horror of war.

Bettie,

I frequently see it intimated in the letters I get from home, that Mother is feeble, and that she is declining. I should like to hear, if she travels about the house and yard—or if she is laid up in the house or bed. Or at least should like to hear of the particulars for satisfaction.

I wrote to Father a day or two after the battle giving the news as to our position, and of the battle at Fredericksburg. You can't imagine the appearance of the dead on the ground, the screams of the wounded, which we could only hear after dark when the firing had ceased. You could easily walk on the dead without touching the ground and in places reminded me of logs put in a heap—in a pile as they were shot down when they attempted to come up the Street. I opened on them with four companies. Major Love says I am not afraid of bullets, but they whistled nearer than I wanted them, and one came near ruining my leg.

My wound will soon be well. I have received my scarf, shoes and Boots. The box had been broken open and the Brandy stolen, I was not suffering for the boots as I had a first rate pair of shoes.

My love to Father, Mother and the rest of you.

Your Bro.

John L. Harris

Tobacco

I now have a "city job," as my brother Lee calls it. Teaching and writing certainly are different from farming, no doubt about it. Heck, I seem to spend half my time writing, whether columns for the *Oxford Ledger* or *Durham Herald-Sun*, or books. I have to admit that sitting at my desk writing words on paper is not exactly strenuous. Certainly not in the way that facing a long row of ground leaves of tobacco on a July day with the temperature over ninety degrees is—tobacco wax all over you, your back aching, sweat rolling down parts of your body you'd rather not mention, and it's only 2:00 p.m. and supper is a long time away.

As you can probably tell, I've experienced firsthand the life of a farmer; and yes, it is hard work, but I can truthfully say some of my fondest memories are from my youth, working the farm. Those days have served me well, as most of the jobs I have had are rather manageable compared to farming in terms of physical labor. For example, my wife, Beth, scolds me for mowing the grass during the hottest part of the day, but I explain to her that cutting grass for an hour or two is nothing after you've experienced "priming" tobacco ten hours a day, five days a week during July.

Farmers are so very important to all of us, and it's a real shame that farms, farmers and the farming life are all on the decline. Most of you who do farm, or have farmed, know why this decline is taking place much better than I do, so I won't try to explain. But the fact is that Oxford and Granville County were ostensibly built through the agricultural products and labor of our farming ancestors, and farmers still play a vital role in our lives.

Let me give you a sketch of what it was like to be raised on a tobacco farm, drawn from memories of my days as basically a "field hand" during my teen years. Literally by the time my spindly legs could reach the brake

A Chesterfield cigarette float takes part in an Oxford Parade. *Photo courtesy of Granville County Historical Society Museum.*

A Granville County tobacco farmer watches the temperature rise in his barn. *Photo courtesy of Granville County Historical Society Museum.*

A little Granville County girl helps out as she handles tobacco leaves.

A young man from Granville County is holding a recently "primed" stick of tobacco.

A hearty meal sure looks good after a hard day's work on a farm in rural Granville County.

pedals on our Farmall tractor, I was put to use delivering trailers of tobacco from the field to the barn, and then taking an empty trailer back to the field to be filled again. Of course, being a young boy, I used my bag of tricks to make my job more interesting. I knew where all the berry patches were on the side of the farm roads, so I was caught once or twice sitting on the tractor with the motor off, stuffing myself with sweet red berries and blueberries as the tobacco primers waited in the hot field for their trailer. I sometimes took naps while driving as the hot sun beat down on me, once taking down part of a pasture fence.

Sometimes while driving the tractor I would daydream about hitting a home run in Yankee Stadium—baseball was and is a passion of mine—and, subsequently, I didn't always do a great job. One morning, and this is a true story, I plowed an entire field of tobacco and was really proud of myself as my father and a neighbor walked toward me. Apparently, while driving the tractor that morning and dreaming of being the next Mickey Mantle or Pete Rose, I had plowed my neighbor's entire field while thinking it was my dad's.

Another time, I got to the field before the "primers" reached the end of the row. It took them awhile, and once there, they couldn't find me. They searched everywhere, and finally one of them saw my big feet sticking out from under the trailer, where I was fast asleep.

Jonah and Marie Milton are headed for the warehouse with a load of tobacco. *Photo courtesy of Donnie and Linda Milton.*

Billy and Mary Wayne Bowling are shown on their farm in the Stem community.

The author driving a tractor on the farm in Providence at age six.

It's strange what one remembers, but to this day one of my proudest moments was when my older brother, Lee, and I got into a "lifting contest" in a field one day. To Lee's consternation, I was able to shoulder a heavy bag of fertilizer from the ground that he could not. I'll never forget the looks and giggles the older men gave me.

I still remember days when farmers in their trucks would be lined up, one after the other, down the streets of Oxford, waiting to sell tobacco in one of the many warehouses in and around town. Everywhere you went downtown you could smell the sweet aroma of cured tobacco.

Sam Ragan was born in Berea as a son of a tobacco farmer and eventually became a well-known writer and poet, being named North Carolina's Poet Laureate. Mr. Ragan wrote the following poem called "The Farmer."

Looking Back

The Farmer

I have seen sunrise.
I have seen moonrise
From these fields.
You know the old saying:
A farmer works from sun to sun,
A woman's work is never done.
And there's a lot of truth in that.
I have seen her face grow old and tired,
And I ain't what I used to be.
But I love to see things grow.
There have been some good years,
Along with the bad, and there's nothing
Better than looking out over
Green growing fields.
There's something about the land
Which gets inside you and it stays
With you the rest of your life.
This land has been in my family
For over a hundred years.
I sure do hate to lose it.

To the Moon

On October 7, 1906, in the rural community of Tally Ho, near Stem, a little boy was born. This Granville County boy would grow up to do wonderful things for the United States, and indeed the world. He would be praised by presidents—Harry Truman said, "[He] is one of my trusted counselors…whose advice is always sound." In 2013, a telescope unlike any other ever built in the world, at a cost estimated to be over $2 billion, will be launched bearing his name.

James Webb was born to John Frederick Webb and Sarah Gorham Webb. J.F. Webb High School is named for John Frederick, who was a longtime Granville school administrator. James graduated from Oxford High School in 1923. He eventually became vice-president of Sperry Gyroscope in Brooklyn, before serving in World War II. From 1946 to 1949, Webb served as director of the U.S. Bureau of the Budget, and from 1949 to 1952 as undersecretary of state, both positions under President Harry Truman.

In 1961 President John Kennedy had a vision of landing on the moon, and he appointed Webb as his administrator of NASA (National Aeronautics and Space Administration). Under Webb's stewardship, NASA sent unmanned spacecrafts to Mars and Venus, giving America its first look ever at outer space. During his tenure at NASA from 1961 to 1968, Webb was in charge of over thirty-five thousand NASA employees. President Lyndon Johnson praised Webb as "the best administrator I've got," and chief justice of the Supreme Court, Warren Burger, said, "I count Jim Webb as one of the people from whom I have learned the most about effective management."

It was in 1969 that Neil Armstrong became the first man to step on the moon, saying the famous words, "One step for man, one giant leap for mankind." Even though James Webb had left office, Webb is regarded today as the man who is most responsible for this historic moment. Congressman

L.H. Fountain said, "For the first time since the beginning of the world there are now footprints on the moon, and the major share of the credit goes to a distinguished son of Granville County, James E. Webb."

Think about it. Go out into your yard tonight, or step on the back porch, and look up at the moon. Look at it from Oxford, from Stem, from Stovall, from wherever you are. It should make us extremely proud that one of our own, a fellow Granville Countian, was the driving force behind man walking on the moon. It makes one wonder if young James, while riding around Oxford some night back in the 1920s perhaps, looked up at the moon and thought that maybe, just maybe, that bright, glowing lunar landscape over two hundred thousand miles away might have special meaning for him in the future.

Five years from now the James Webb Space Telescope will be launched, succeeding the famous Hubble Space Telescope. This spacecraft will travel farther into the universe than any other in the history of the world, sending back images never seen by humans, and it will do so bearing the name of James Webb. Sean O'Keefe, who was NASA administrator at the time of the naming of this telescope, said this about Webb: "It is fitting that Hubble's successor be named in honor of James Webb. Thanks to his efforts, we got our first glimpses at the dramatic landscape of outer space. He took our nation on its first voyages of exploration, turning our imagination into reality."

James Webb passed away in 1992 and is now buried in Arlington National Cemetery.

A Good Man

What a joy it must have been for this little boy. Up high in the Granville County Courthouse, this boy, eight years old, pulled on the rope with all his might to ring the bell in celebration. Over and over he rang the bell, sending its merry sounds into the air and over Main Street, down Williamsboro Street, up Hillsboro Street and over and beyond College Street. On the streets of downtown Oxford, a crowd estimated to be in the thousands was "hoopin' and hollerin'"—hats were tossed in the air, friends slapped each other on the back, people danced on the sidewalks. Hardly anyone was drunk, because as the young boy later in life remembered, "no one could afford to buy a drink."

The year was 1932, and Franklin Delano Roosevelt had just been elected president. The Great Depression had taken jobs, closed banks, made food scarce on many tables and generally sapped people's spirits. These were tough times in Oxford, Stem, Stovall, Berea, Creedmoor, Oak Hill, Wilton, Providence, Tally Ho, Bullock and the surrounding farms and communities of Granville, along with most regions of the country. But now that FDR had been elected, there was hope for better times. After all, a man could cling to hope—he could go forward with determination if he thought better times awaited him and his family.

So on this November night of 1932, high up in the historic Granville County Courthouse, which in that year was already ninety-two years old, having been built in 1840, little Arthur Ray Currin rang the bell time after time. The election returns were coming in, and FDR was winning easily. Frank Hancock, who represented Granville County in the United States House of Representatives from 1930 to 1939, kept track of the election returns on a big chalkboard in the courthouse. Hancock would later serve in the FDR presidency as head of the Farm Security Administration.

In 1946, fourteen years after taking part in the joyous celebration in Oxford, Arthur Ray Currin would be in another courthouse, witnessing one of the most famous trials in history. The place was Nuremburg, Germany, and Nazi war criminals such as Hermann Göring, Rudolf Hess and Joachim von Ribbentrop were standing trial for their atrocities during World War II. Arthur Ray Currin was attending the trial as a soldier of the United States Army. Mr. Currin still remembers the sights and sounds of this trial in the Nuremburg Palace of Justice, recalling that Göring sat on a bench with a disdainful smile on his face, and Hess remained stone-faced throughout the proceedings.

Arthur Ray Currin was born in 1924 in the Oak Hill Township in the Wilbourns Store area. His parents were Joe and Beatrice West Currin. Joe was a farmer, a Granville County deputy sheriff and also ran a country store. Mr. Currin married his wife Marie in February 1945 and just a couple of weeks later boarded an ocean liner bound for Europe to do his duty in World War II. Marie eventually would retire from teaching science and home economics at Oak Hill, Creedmoor, J.F. Webb and D.N. Hix, after a long and successful career in the Granville County school system.

Mr. Currin joined the 103rd Infantry Division in France, and was part of the last big push of the war. The 103rd took part in the 1945 spring offensive, pushing into Germany, across the Rhine and on through Austria. Among other ribbons and citations, Mr. Currin was awarded the Bronze Star Medal and the Combat Infantry Badge, with the latter award for outstanding performance of duty with the 103rd Infantry Division in ground combat.

After the war, Mr. Currin came back to his family's farm—the Currin family has owned the land since the late 1800s. In 1953, Sheriff Roy Jones asked Arthur Ray to fill a deputy sheriff position. Mr. Currin declined, saying that he would not have time due to his farming. Sheriff Jones then replied, "How about just helping me out until I can do better?" Mr. Currin, being a man with a strong sense of duty, said that he would help Sheriff Jones for awhile. Little did he know that this conversation would lead to a thirty-year career in law enforcement. Mr. Currin was a deputy sheriff from 1953 to 1963, then when Granville County voted "wet" in 1963, he became the county ABC (Alcoholic Beverage Control) chief, staying in that position until 1980. From 1980 to 1986 he served as sheriff of Granville County.

Along with many other law enforcement duties, Mr. Currin was responsible for enforcing liquor laws, which involved busting numerous "moonshine" operations. The mid-1960s were the high point of moonshining in Granville County. Tactics used by Mr. Currin and his assistants were the "element of surprise" and "good informants," and also "good running legs" to chase down moonshiners caught by surprise. Archie Wilkins, who assisted

Granville County law enforcement officers have just busted another liquor still. *Photo courtesy of Granville County Historical Society Museum.*

in many of these "still-busting operations," could "run like the wind," and Wilkins chased down quite a few moonshiners. Mr. Currin ran down some himself, recalling one incident where he "chased a fellow through the woods and way down a tobacco row" before tackling him.

Cynthia Currin, Mr. Currin's daughter, wrote a fascinating article on her father and moonshining for the April 2000 edition of *Carolina Country* magazine. In the article, Cynthia wrote about her father and his assistants performing a raid—how they arrested the still workers, dynamited the still and poured out the liquor. One bust that Cynthia wrote about was the largest still Mr. Currin raided in Granville County, with a mash capacity of twenty thousand gallons, in which they confiscated fifteen thousand pounds of unused sugar and donated it to the county schools.

If you would like to see a real liquor still, visit the Granville County Historical Society Museum in Oxford. You can see the still and some of the equipment moonshiners used to make their "homemade brew," and there is a huge picture that covers a wall of Mr. Currin and his assistants "busting a still."

Now eighty-three years old and still going strong, Mr. Currin remains on the same farm where he was born. Although he was a law enforcement officer for much of his life, a decorated military soldier and a merchant who

Sherriff Roy Jones (with glasses) is squatting on the dam. Pictured in the background, from left to right, are Arthur Ray Currin, Bernard Newton, Wallace Bowling and Tom Clayton. These men have just busted a Granville County liquor still. *Photo courtesy of Arthur Ray Currin.*

Arthur Ray Currin with wife, Marie. *Photo courtesy of Arthur Ray Currin.*

helped his father Joe run their country store, farming was always special to his heart. He still stays very busy on the farm, with fields to mow, government programs to cooperate with, pine trees to look after, a garden to tend with wife, Marie, growing and picking grapes and canning tomatoes and jelly. Mr. and Mrs. Currin have four children—daughter Cynthia, and sons Ted, Tom and Tim. Mr. Currin also enjoys reading and discussing Granville County history and attending American Legion and army reunion events.

Granville County can truly be proud of citizens such as Mr. Currin. I am looked at sometimes as somewhat of a "county historian," but I admit without hesitation that I have learned most of what little I know from people like Arthur Ray Currin, who has "lived the history" about which I write. Mr. Currin, when told I was writing this, told me more than once not to "build me up, don't fluff anything, I'm just an old farmer." Well, Mr. Currin, this story is not fluffed up in any way. It is just about a good man who has lived his life well, and for that you deserve our gratitude.

Camp Butner

We have a new town in Granville County. Yes, Butner has been with us since 1942, when Camp Butner was built by the United States government as a training base and prisoner of war camp during World War II. But very recently, largely through the efforts of our state representative, Jim Crawford, state senator, Doug Berger, and Oxford attorney, Jim Wrenn, Butner was officially incorporated as a new town, no longer run by the state.

I thought now would be a good time for us to remember how Butner got started, with the creation of Camp Butner. The following article was written by Jim Wise for the *Durham Herald-Sun* in 2002. Jim now writes a history column for the *Durham News*, a publication of the *Raleigh News and Observer*. He helped me with the Camp Butner chapter of my *Granville County: Images of America* book. The following excerpts of his article on Camp Butner are reprinted here with his permission. Also, Eddie Smith of Butner has written a great book on Camp Butner called *Voices From the Field*.

That winter of 1942, Luke Veasey was going to high school in Creedmoor. From home, he would walk three miles to Cozart Station to catch the bus for the five-mile ride to school; then repeat the process vice versa in the afternoon.

This particular afternoon, when Luke came walking past the old Veasey graveyard and up the road toward Veasey Ridge, he saw a strange car at the edge of their yard. A man was sitting inside the car.

Luke's father, Kinch Veasey, sat on their porch, holding a shotgun.

"You see that man in the car?" the elder Veasey said. "If he steps out, I'm gonna shoot him."

Matters never got to the point of shooting. Not that it would have mattered if they had, mattered any more than the neighbor's sign:

NOTICE
LAND POSTED
I FORBID ANY MAN
TRESPASSING ON THIS
LAND
J.W. Carpenter

If fighting City Hall is an exercise in futility, what can you call fighting the Law, the Courthouse, the Army and the powers of multiple city halls besides? You can get your shotgun and stand your ground, but when the government man comes calling…

"We didn't move," said Luke Veasey. "Daddy told him he didn't have anywhere to go and they hadn't given him any money and he wasn't going to move.

"They gave us thirty days. And we didn't move, and they gave us another thirty days. And we didn't move, and they gave us another thirty days."

By then, it was March, time to be working the land for crops. A cousin also condemned to move, Grady Veasey, remembers the family story.

"He wasn't going," Grady Veasey said.

"They said, 'You are going, too.'

"He moved, and they burned his house the next day."

Because the Japanese had come and the war had come and then Uncle Sam had come—for forty thousand acres, more or less, of his country around the junction of Granville, Person and Durham counties.

The nation needed yet another base, for training infantry and for a hospital to tend wounded from Europe—especially the head cases, shell shock. So, if your people had been on that land for two hundred years; or if you were landless and had nowhere to go; or if the government had just helped you spend years getting your land in prime growing shape, that was just too bad for you. Maybe the government men would let you buy it back, after everything was finished.

That didn't work out, either, in most cases, and the state of North Carolina ended up with the greatest chunk of old Camp Butner. Some of the farmers did buy their land back after World War II. But by then, most had moved on and were well into new lives and different places. Or they just didn't want to go back where it hurt.

This time, sixty years ago, Camp Butner was a name on plans for a triangle of countryside; rolling low hills, pinewoods, creeks; churches, graveyards, tenant shanties and substantial homes of brick or lumber; crossroads

Addie Howard teaching her class at Knap of Reeds School in 1942. This school would soon be torn down to make way for Camp Butner.

communities with names like Wilkins, Cozart, Copley's Corner, Shoofly and Shake-Rag; and farms dotting the good cropland.

Six months later, it would be a small city ready for thirty-five thousand residents, complete with streets, sewers, reservoir, telephone exchange, store, theater, churches, gym, machine shops—and obstacle courses and firing range.

In the process, about 425 families had moved. Eight church congregations disbanded. Five schools closed. Bodies were exhumed from 1,638 graves and removed to a new federal cemetery; some cemeteries, judged out-of-the-way, were left alone and families of those interred were issued special visiting passes.

"The United States government contracted to relocate all the burials within the Butner reservation," said the Rev. Eddie Smith, a retired minister who published a book on the camp, *Voices from the Field*, for the town of Butner's fiftieth anniversary in 1992.

After the anniversary, Smith headed a project to identify any cemeteries within the military reservation. He and his helpers found twenty-eight—abandoned, forgotten, desecrated.

One, which had belonged to the Knap of Reeds Baptist Church, lay beneath a cattle barn at a state agriculture station.

"This was quite a community," Smith said, looking from the side of the Old Oxford Highway—Old North Carolina 75—toward the barn, which dominated a hillock. "A Methodist church was across the road, and a Masonic Hall. Peeds and Tilleys lived here. We moved sixty graves from here. And many we could never find."

They also found the remains of tombstones, shattered during construction work.

For some residents of Grandurson—a term coined by *Durham Sun* reporter Ben Patrick, denoting the affected regions of GRANville, DURham and PerSON counties—the first inkling of their future came in the newspaper on May 8, 1941: "Granville County Site Is Considered For Huge New Army Training Center."

That the land in question had lately suffered from tobacco wilt, and that the vicinity offered "excellence in recreational features," were selling points to get the army and the construction jobs and the $500,000 weekly GI payroll a base would bring. Blighted cropland would go cheap, movies and churches and beer joints would keep soldiers happy.

"Everybody around was excited, except the people who lived there," said A.W. Teasley. "They were dumbstruck.

"Most were tenants, most had nowhere to go. Some landowners were happy about it, some it just about killed."

Actually, another site had been considered, farther east in Granville County, near Wilton. It was abandoned in the face of local opposition.

Out in the country, as summer and events moved on, a movement was organizing. On August 12, 2000, residents met at Stem Schoolhouse in Granville County, and drew up a petition against the camp. Another, similar petition collected 194 signatures. Both were circulated, to no effect.

On January 29, 1942, Butner Project Manager Robert Downey met with about one hundred Grandurson residents at the Knap of Reeds Baptist Church. He told them that U.S. marshals would deliver "Declarations of Taking" in the next two days.

"You take a family of rabbits and scatter them about the countryside. They don't come to nothing. Human beings are like that. You scatter us and we'll just go down," said Merritt Duke of Granville County in July 1941.

Camp Butner did bring its benefits. For a while, there were jobs that paid up to $1.25 an hour—at a time the going minimum was thirty-five cents. Creedmoor became a busy place, serving the construction force. GI wives and children rented rooms to be close to their husbands and fathers. Durham was swarmed by as many as four thousand off-duty GIs on any given day; one wartime Saturday, every liquor store in town was sold out before noon.

"Everyone around the perimeter just about, where I lived, got work at Camp Butner, building," said A.W. Teasley. "It meant a whole lot to them… At that time, it was a good thing in that area for sure."

Teasley himself left a thirty-five-cent job at a sawmill to make $18 a week at the camp. "Really, just walking, probably ten miles a day." He worked all the summer of '42, laying streets and running power lines.

Teasley would never go back to the farm life he grew up with.

"I farmed all my life, from the time I was big enough to help to 1940," he said. "It was a rough life back then."

In 1932, Teasley's father made a profit of $27 on his investment of $400 and a year's labor to raise tobacco. Across the three-county region, most of the farms were eight to ten acres, "two-mule" spreads. That was all a man could handle.

"Farmers back then, if you had bread on the table, you were lucky."

Nowadays, what remains of the Camp Butner headquarters is a huge brick chimney in a stand of pine trees off a back street in the town of Butner, which itself is a ward of the state of North Carolina. A row of tall, square smokestacks without buildings marks the location of vehicle repair shops that could handle anything from a Jeep to a tank. The old recreation hall is a community center, and the old John Forsyth home, used as a stockade for GIs who came back to camp drunk, looks down upon a "Welcome to Butner" sign.

Sixty years ago, 425 families, and all that went with them, were being moved out of the way of big events and powerful forces. Moved out of the way of history in the making, you might say; or you might say that these were some of the earliest victims of America's Second World War.

Sixty years later, relics remain around the old camp: the Butner Catholic Church was a base chapel; homes are built from barracks lumber; good works are done at the hospital built to treat the head cases coming back from Europe; a barren strip in the woods marks the spot where loads of surplus weapons were buried in preservative salt.

And where roots ran deep, memories run long. "They treated people pretty shabby," said Luke Veasey.

It would be almost two years before the Veaseys saw any pay for the land the army took, and then it was only half the contracted price. It was more months to get the rest, and all they had offered was $10,500 for 254 acres plus barn and everything. The timber alone had appraised at more than that, and the army wouldn't let them cut it.

"They wouldn't let anyone cut it, do anything. I went to a neighbor's house, two old maids and a bachelor, and the price they offered them—they were crying like babies. They didn't have anywhere to go."

The November 21, 1942 edition of the *State* magazine carried an article titled "Here is Camp Butner." The article ran over three pages, crowing about the base's up-to-dateness, its huge capacities and its readiness to make boys into fighting men.

About those who had gone before, there was not a word.

A Great Victory
for Stem High School

Back in 1936, the Stem High School boys' basketball team beat Creedmoor High School for the Granville County Championship. Now, this might surprise some of you, as there is no longer a Stem High or Creedmoor High. But what these young country boys from Stem did a few nights later really did Granville County proud. They went to Chapel Hill and laid a whipping on the University of North Carolina Tarheels.

Before the Granville County basketball tournament of 1936, Coach Pegram of Stem High School promised his team that if they won the tournament, he would take them to see a college team play. Well, during these years of depression and limited travel, this promise from their coach really excited these Stem youngsters. Heck, a weekend trip to Oxford was considered a big thing.

Now believe it or not, Stem had to beat three other teams to win the championship, but here is what is quite remarkable…they beat Wilton High School, Berea High School and Creedmoor High School all in the same day. That's right, at 11:00 a.m. Stem beat Wilton, ate a light lunch and beat Berea at 2:00 p.m., then took a school bus back to Stem for supper, came back to Creedmoor and defeated Creedmoor High at 7:00 p.m.

Brent Meadows played on this 1936 Stem team, and recalls these years of playing basketball like it was yesterday. In just a few months Mr. Meadows will turn ninety, and this longtime Oxford resident is still going strong and is a real pleasure to talk to. He is a man Oxford should be very proud of, having been a successful businessman and farmer, an active member of the community and a good husband and father.

According to Meadows, Creedmoor had defeated Stem twice in the 1936 season prior to the tournament. Just some of the names of the Creedmoor players could put a little scare into an opposing team. They had a "Rip"

The Stem High School team that beat the University of North Carolina Tarheels.

Roberts, a "Big'un" Bullock and, according to Mr. Meadows, "a great big fella" in "Hen" Clay. Understand, back in this time there was a huge rivalry among county teams, so when the staff at Creedmoor offered to feed the Stem team supper before their big game against each other, no chances were taken. Mamie Daniel, with the Stem team in Creedmoor, liked to feed her boys properly in her capacity as lunchroom supervisor. So perhaps sensing that the Creedmoor folks might be up to something, such as serving her boys some overly rich food that might upset their stomachs and hinder their ability to play well, Mamie told Coach Pegram of Stem to turn the offer down. The Stem boys took a bus back to Stem and ate their own home cooked food, not taking a chance on the Creedmoor cuisine.

After filling their bellies, the Stem team rode back to Creedmoor ready for their third game of the day. After all, playing three games of basketball in a day wasn't so hard. Most of the boys spent many a day in the hot sun farming tobacco and other crops. No, these country lads could play basketball all day long.

With the promise of the trip to see the Tarheels play still on their minds, Stem beat Creedmoor to claim the county championship. Stem had some talent, with Brent Meadows and his fine dribbling and passing skills, and they had quite a "big fella," themselves in Wallace Bowling to combat big "Hen" Clay of Creedmoor. Bowling stood a good six feet three or six feet four inches tall. Also "Bunk" Guthrie of Stem could shoot like nobody around the county. According to Mr. Meadows, "That Guthrie boy was a little bitty boy. He didn't farm and work like the rest of us. He just played ball all the time. He'd shoot balls all day long." In the end, "Bunk" and the boys from Stem beat "Big'un," "Rip," "Hen" and the rest of the Creedmoor boys. On to Chapel Hill.

Coach Pegram piled his team into his car and arrived at the UNC gym, where a full house awaited the game between UNC and Wake Forest. Word came that the Wake Forest team could not make it due to snowy conditions. Disappointed fans started to leave the gym. Coach Pegram ran to the UNC coach and told him "Heck, all these people want to see a game. My boys can stir up a game for you." UNC agreed, thinking at least they would get a little workout playing somebody and it would also maybe give the fans something to see. UNC supplied the Stem team with pants and shoes, and the boys stripped down to their T-shirts.

The freshmen team of UNC started the game, but by halftime the game was very close. Wanting to teach the high school boys a lesson, some of the varsity players for the Tarheels played the second half. Brent Meadows recalls that, "They thought they'd beat the soup out of us country boys." But they didn't.

The game was tied with a few seconds to go. It was Stem's ball. Mr. Meadows recalls that he brought the ball upcourt, and "Bunk" Guthrie "received a pass and somewhere between that center line and the foul line he shot it, and the ball ripped right through the net."

The crowd sat in stunned silence; then roared with approval. They couldn't believe what they had witnessed. Little Stem High School had beaten the mighty Tarheels. "I've never heard such a roar," says Brent Meadows today. As news spread that night around Granville County, the Stem boys were treated as heroes. "At school, you couldn't hardly live with us for a few days," says Meadows. They were proud of what they had done, and we are proud of them today.

Thad Stem

Rising early in the morning, he would leave his old stately house on Front Street with a goodbye to his beautiful wife Marguerite. Across the road to Main Street this native of Oxford would go, walking briskly and with a purpose to his stride. He knew everyone in town, or so it seemed, and most everyone knew him. Not one to ever be at a loss for words, he would greet and be greeted constantly on his two-block walk into downtown Oxford. He would pass the post office, and he stopped there often both for business and pleasure, then would continue on down Main Street past shops, cafés and warehouses stacked to the ceiling with piles of cured tobacco. Upon reaching Hall's Drugstore, at the time the oldest business in Oxford, this man would climb the stairs to the top floor above the drugstore and enter his office.

Once inside this office above Hall's Drugstore on Main Street in Oxford, he would sit at his desk, and amidst a clutter of papers, books, letters, pens, pencils, notepads, paper clips and his trusty typewriter, this native of Oxford created some of the best writing the state of North Carolina has ever produced. His output was prodigious, as he wrote hundreds of columns for the *Oxford Ledger, Raleigh News and Observer, Durham Morning Herald* and *Durham Sun*, among other newspapers. He wrote fine poetry and he also wrote books, seventeen in all. (*Entries from Oxford* is my favorite.)

Thad Stem once said, "Much of what I write is grounded in the feeling that one is what he is because of where he lives." Just as Oxford and Granville County left their imprint on Stem, so did Thad Stem leave his imprint on his native town and county.

Mr. Stem was the son of Thad Stem Sr., one-time mayor of Oxford and a prominent attorney. His father also holds another distinction, especially among local basketball fans. Thad Stem Sr. played on Duke University's first basketball team, and served as captain of that team way back in 1905–06.

Thad Stem, writing another book.

Engaging is the best word I come up with in describing Stem's writing. Read the following excerpt from a story called "Circus Day Tomorrow," and see if you don't agree. It is based on bygone days in Oxford that Stem experienced.

After breakfast, Wesley would go into Oxford and work awhile. Then he'd fetch Martha, his wife, and the boys. The four would look out the windows of his second-story office when the fabulous circus parade came down the street. Each one would wave a balloon from the window, to the parade and to friends crowded and stacked like bright playing cards along the sidewalks and gutters.

They would all eat at the show grounds. The boys would be sea lions with foam on their faces and up their noses in form of cotton candy. They'd eat hot dogs and candy-apples and swill pop until they had to send for the doctor.

When their original balloons busted, Wesley would get a round of new ones, green and gleaming, and yellow and sassy. He'd win Martha a kewpie doll throwing baseballs, and when he swung the sledge, to send the ball up that narrow, metal ladder, why he'd make it bounce off the garden gate of heaven.

It might be better not to go inside the hootch-a-me-kootch-a-me show, but they'd watch the gals dance on the improvised stage in front of the side-show tent. But as the gals shimmied and gyrated, Wesley would think about Martha. She might be pushing forty but she still wore a size ten dress, and he was reasonably sure she was 23 around the middle.

He doubted the barker would say about the leading dancing girl, as the old-time professor said: "She dances first on her right leg and then on her left leg and between the two she makes a handsome living."

Then they would all sit together and watch the ingenious acts and the death-defying acts in the big tent. They would roar with the clowns, but they would peep through their fingers when the girl did the triple somersault on the high trapeze.

And after the final act, Wesley would buy a whole stand of balloons, as many as fifty perhaps. Some balloons they would pop, in the manner of merry vandals, and some they would free, as birds from a cage. But they would give many to friends of all ages, as the four of them walked home down the middle of the street.

Thad Stem's books are still displayed prominently in the Richard Thornton Library, and a large portrait adorns a wall. There is a nice display on Mr. Stem in the Granville County Historical Society Museum, located just behind the old Hall's Drugstore building and the Granville County Courthouse. Mr. Stem is now enshrined in the North Carolina Literary Hall of Fame, and his papers are housed at the University of North Carolina in Chapel Hill.

We should be proud of this great writer who once called Oxford home. Thomas Walters, at the time an English professor at North Carolina State University, wrote the following about Stem's writing: "This state, indeed this country, is richer for Thad Stem Jr. and his stories. More than our praise, he deserves our attention. His work deeply merits it."

Hanging around a Country Store

Old country stores have a very special meaning for me. My next-door neighbor, so to speak, as I grew up was one of these country stores. It was run by my father, O.L. Bowling Jr., in the Providence community. Hanging around this store is one of my fondest memories of growing up. In fact, some of the events I recall seem like they occurred just days ago. Most of these memories are from the 1960s and early to mid-1970s.

Daddy's store seemed to have a little of everything. Not like most country stores of today, where you might buy gas, a pack of cigarettes and a soft drink. No, Daddy's store had those items, but it was also a grocery store. Quite a few people in the Providence area did their grocery shopping in the store, as we had everything from canned goods to frozen chickens, fresh bread to molasses, bags of ice to any kind of ice cream you could want, cans of oil to what we back then called TV dinners, hoops of cheese to sandwiches delivered daily by the Durham Sandwich Company. There was a huge jar of cookies, sold as singles or however many you wanted. Children would come in with their parents and gaze longingly at all the sweet treats, such as honey buns, Baby Ruths and Pepsis. Daddy would often reach into the cookie jar and hand these wide-eyed kids a free snack, or place a pack of Juicy Fruit chewing gum in their hands.

Of course, my friends sometimes thought that I was lucky, assuming I had access to all the candy and drinks I wanted. Not so. Oh, maybe I did get a "sweet treat" a little more often than a kid whose father did not run a store. But it certainly did not mean my brother and sisters and I could gorge ourselves—not even close. I'll tell this story to the embarrassment of my older brother, Lee. It seems one day Lee and I were "helping out" around the store, when Lee developed a taste for some animal crackers. A little too close to supper, Daddy said no. Well, Lee had a hardheaded streak in him,

Shirley Wheeler Currin and Eugene Wheeler are outside the Averette Grocery in Providence in 1953. *Photo courtesy of Lucius and Rowena Wheeler.*

a trait which some say continues to this day. So when Daddy walked outside to pump some gas, Lee's taste for animal crackers got the best of him. He grabbed a box and held them on the side of his body away from Daddy's vision, or so he thought. Out the door he went toward the house. Well, Daddy saw him, called him over and "popped him on the head" rather well, in full view of a few customers. The old boy hasn't had a fondness for animal crackers since.

I developed a distaste for chewing tobacco. Harry Gold Wheeler, who had quite a reputation for his barbecue chicken, sometimes helped Daddy at the store. One day, while Harry Gold wasn't looking, Lee, Gary Jones, Brin Wilkins and I grabbed a pack of chewing tobacco. Taking it behind the store, we all tried some. I can only recall my nearly throwing up, deciding right then that was a habit the grownups could keep for themselves. Now Brin is the chief deputy sheriff of Granville County, so we must excuse this little childhood transgression.

Two things really gave me trouble once I started to run the register. I have never been very mechanical, so when customers wanted a gas fill up and their oil checked, I would take forever to find the oil stick. Also, we sold huge

Al Woodlief, the current mayor of Oxford, is shown at one and a half years old with his mother, Mozelle Milton Woodlief, at Davis Averette Country Store near Oxford.

quantities of cigarettes and literally had stacks and stacks to choose from. If someone wanted a pack of Winstons, you had Winston filtered, Winston not filtered, Winston Lights, Winston regular, Winston 100s, etc.—and always with a book of matches. Half the time the customer ended up telling me where they were.

I remember fondly sitting around with the local men of the community, as they would use the store to rest, socialize, catch up and "get away from the wife" for a few moments. Little did they know their dear wives were happy to have them gone! I even remember what they ate and other tendencies. Brindell Wilkins, Brin's daddy and a good neighbor, loved his small coke (six-ounce bottle) and oatmeal cookies; James Clayborne ate many a Nutty Buddy ice cream; Brooks Green liked his Pepsis; and Jonah Milton always got $5 of gas. Euryl Thorpe would lunch heartily on a can of pork and beans, sardines and a pack of crackers, and "Uncle Sweet" Taborn, as he was affectionately called by everyone, would drink one sixteen-ounce Pepsi after another. Everybody loved Harold Green, who would grab a tall Schlitz a couple times a day and leave the money on the counter. Calvin helped out around the store, and whenever one of my squeamish sisters would come by, he would pop out his glass eye, place it in his cap and chase them around the store with it.

It was simply amazing how men in the store would transform into saints once a lady walked in. They would sit up straight and their language would suddenly be suitable for church. But they were all good people, such as James Satterwhite, Moses Averett, who could beat anybody in checkers, Brodie Jones, a man so friendly he would seem to hang half his body out his car window to wave at you, and Ralph Morgan, who farmed with us and whom I will always think of when I think of big, strong men. Ralph seemed to never tire, and had the biggest hands I've ever seen. All he seemed to require was his pack of Kool cigarettes from Daddy's store.

The country store of my early years was a good place to be, full of vivid and pleasant memories. It was a gathering place, a place to refresh oneself, to swap a tale or two. Some of this still goes on, I'm sure, but I think I prefer my country store memories of years back. "Looking Back" on them still gives me great pleasure.

A World War II Experience

Colonel Danny Bowling, a native of Granville County and graduate of Oxford High School, retired from the Army National Guard on October 31, 2003, with thirty-seven years of service. The first seventeen years of his career were as a traditional guardsman, and the last twenty years were active duty.

Colonel Bowling's career included eighteen years of troop duty, culminating as a battalion commander. The remaining years of his career were served in various assignments on the adjutant general's staff. These positions included the director of information management, the director of the Office of Military Support to Civil Authorities, which involved working with the governor and FEMA during natural disasters, and the last four years as the director of logistics for statewide operations.

His last two duty assignments were at Fort Riley, Kansas, and Fort Irwin, California, where he prepared the Thirtieth Infantry Brigade for deployment to Iraq.

The following story is about Wallace Bowling, who was Danny's father. Wallace witnessed one of the most historical events of the twentieth century as a soldier in World War II. Wallace was my uncle, whom I remember as a tall, strong man who always seemed happy to see me. Wallace's two brothers, Billy and O.L., also served in World War II. Danny Bowling wrote the following about his father, Wallace:

> *In 1943, Sergeant Wallace D. Bowling, a native of the Stem community of Granville County, was stationed at Nellis Air Force Base in Las Vegas, Nevada. He had recently sent for his sweetheart, Ella Greene of the Dexter Community, to travel by train to Las Vegas so that they could marry before he shipped overseas.*

Wallace Bowling is in his World War II uniform. Standing beside him is younger brother O.L. Bowling Jr. *Photo courtesy of Mary Bowling.*

They did marry and settled in a small cottage near Nellis with a small backyard. Wallace, being a farm boy, decided to plant a garden. His father, Ollie Bowling, mailed him some vegetable seeds, and also some very special Granville County tobacco seeds. Wallace had a fine garden and also probably the only tobacco crop ever grown in Las Vegas. Soldiers throughout the base came to the Bowling garden to see what tobacco looked like.

The honeymoon lasted less than a year, and then Wallace received his orders to ship to the Tinian Island in the South Pacific near Guam. Ella had to pack all their belongings in a 1940 Ford and drive back to Granville County. This wasn't an easy task considering there were not any interstates, only two-lane roads from Las Vegas to Oxford.

Another Granville County native, Elbert Blackwell, was also shipped to the Tinian Island along with Wallace. Little did Wallace or Elbert know they were about to become a part of history.

The Tinian Island had been captured from the Imperial Japanese Army. As a result, the American B29 bombers would be able to fly from Tinian Island to Japan and return on a tank of fuel.

It instantly became a strategic location for the Army Air Corp to establish an airfield. Tinian is at the southern end of the Mariana Islands and Tinian itself is about twelve miles long and five miles wide.

Most of the coastline consists of sheer cliffs of rusty brown lava rising from the sea. Since the Tinian airfield was hastily built, accommodations were crude, but compared to the infantry acceptable. The rule for housing was twelve officers or twenty enlisted men in a Quonset hut, twenty-nine feet wide by fifty feet long.

Tinian, although small and crude, had just become the most valuable real estate owned by the 20th Air Force. It was August of 1945, Germany had been defeated and the American campaign to secure Okinawa from the Japanese had just ended.

It had taken over five hundred thousand American troops three months to secure Okinawa and the casualties were tremendous: 49,151 American soldiers dead plus 36 warships sunk and 332 badly damaged.

More than 109,000 Japanese were killed. President Truman and the American military leadership knew an invasion of the Japanese mainland would be the most costly loss of lives of any invasion of mankind and it was time to unleash the American secret to end the war, the atomic bomb.

At 2:45 a.m., on August 6, 1945, the B29 bomber, the Enola Gay, took off from the north runway from Tinian. The Enola Gay was piloted by Colonel Paul Tibbets, who had named the plane after his mother. Her takeoff weight was 150,000 pounds; the 65 ton Enola Gay with 7,000 gallons of fuel, a 12-man crew and a 5-ton atomic bomb.

She was overloaded by fifteen thousand pounds and had to use every inch of the runway to get airborne.

Wallace and Elbert were there as the Enola Gay rose to the sky. Later that day Japan would be hit with the most powerful bomb invented by man up to 1945.

At 8:15 a.m., after a flight of five and a half hours, the crew of the Enola Gay dropped the atomic bomb on Hiroshima. Again on August 9, 1945, the second atomic bomb, in a B29, took off from Tinian with its target of Nagasaki.

With the dropping of these two bombs, the Japanese surrendered. The Japanese toll was heavy with more than 132,000 people dead or missing. Many more died later from the effects of atomic radiation.

Although tragic for the Japanese people, thousands of allied and American lives were spared as an invasion of Japan never occurred. For many Americans, Pearl Harbor was finally avenged.

In January 1946, following the end of World War II, First Sergeant Wallace Bowling returned to Oxford to his wife Ella and his new son Danny who was born while he was deployed. He immediately started a career of farming, which remained his passion for the remainder of his life.

Wallace grew approximately one hundred acres of tobacco each year from the 1960s into the 1990s. He was also a part-time deputy with the Granville County Sheriff's Department. Wallace and Ella had two other children, Ronnie and Vicki.

Granville County People

FRANK HANCOCK

Frank Hancock was born in Oxford in 1894. After serving in both the North Carolina House of Representatives and the state senate, Hancock became a member of the United States House of Representatives in 1930, where he served until 1939. In 1943, Hancock was appointed director of the Farm Security Administration during Franklin Roosevelt's presidency. He also practiced law and became a judge in Granville County. Hancock died in 1969 and is buried in Elmwood Cemetery in Oxford.

RAYMOND HARRIS

Raymond Harris, due to an accident earlier in his life, became totally blind in 1933. Not one to accept pity, Harris got permission to set up a small "store" in front of the Granville County Courthouse. He started with an old piano box and $30 of stock, and sold tobacco products, packaged cakes and crackers. Soon after a refrigerated drink box was added.

Harris, through politeness, friendly customer service and gift of conversation, developed his business to a considerable degree. School-children, courthouse workers, downtown merchants and shoppers and farmers would stop by Harris's business, which became known as the Blue Dot, to get a pack of cigarettes or a cold Coke and enjoy a chat with Harris. The Blue Dot became one of Oxford's most popular destinations. Raymond Harris, the man without the gift of sight, did much to make Oxford a friendly atmosphere for its citizens and visitors.

T.G. STEM

T.G. Stem, from Oxford, graduated from Trinity College, now called Duke University. In 1905, Stem played on the first basketball team in Duke's history, and served as the first captain in Duke basketball's history. Stem became mayor of Oxford in 1913, then served admirably in World War I. After the war, Stem returned to Oxford and was elected mayor again. Stem's son, Thad Stem, became a famous writer, and is profiled elsewhere in this book.

FRANK SLAUGHTER

Frank Slaughter grew up on a tobacco farm in Berea. He graduated from Oxford High School in 1922 at the age of fourteen, and then entered

Trinity College, which is now Duke University. This young genius graduated from Duke at the age of seventeen. He then went to Johns Hopkins, where he received his MD. After being a successful doctor, Slaughter turned to writing. Over a long career, he wrote sixty-two books that sold over sixty million copies. Several of his books were turned into films, including *Doctor's Wives*, in which Dyan Cannon and Gene Hackman starred in 1971.

Frank Slaughter.

CLARENCE BAILEY

Clarence Bailey was known around Granville County as "The Sage of Oak Hill." Bailey was known for his ability to predict the future. People from around the county sought Bailey out, many driving to his home in a sparsely populated section of the county, some twelve miles from Oxford. When Bailey came to Oxford, he would be surrounded by citizens wanting him to tell them their fortune. Bailey would pull out his magnifying glass, which he always carried, and scrutinize the person's palm while asking questions such as when a person was born.

Uncannily accurate, Bailey once predicted that Duke would defeat the University of North Carolina by the score of 13 to 3 in football, with Carolina scoring first and Duke then scoring twice to win. That is exactly how the game ended. Bailey was in constant demand for parties, barbecues and picnics. Not only able to seemingly predict the future, Bailey was quite a philosopher, able to quote lines from classics and from the Bible.

ROBERT POTTER

Robert Potter was born in Granville County in 1799. He became a sought-after lawyer in Oxford after starting his practice in 1821. His personality was so striking, his features so captivating and his charm so commanding that a crowd always assembled about him when he appeared in public. He served in the United States Congress and was elected once while confined to the county jail. Potter, having a fiery temper, castrated two men for sleeping with his wife—or so he believed. At the time there was no law against castration, or what came to be called "Potterizing." The following year, the North Carolina legislature passed the Potter Act, making castration a felony. Potter would serve six months in jail and was fined one thousand dollars.

Controversy continued to follow Potter. In 1835 he was expelled from the North Carolina House of Commons for "cheating at cards." Somewhat in disgrace, Potter moved to Texas, got involved in state politics and later was appointed secretary of the Texas Navy. Potter County in Texas is named for this Granville County native.

JAMES HORNER

Horner Military Academy once graced what is now Military Street in Oxford. James Horner founded the school, and his son, Jerome Horner, taught at the school for many years. Among many famous graduates were Locke Craig, a future governor of North Carolina; state Supreme Court justices W.A. Devin and Wallace Winbourne; J. Crawford Biggs and John Morris, both future solicitors general of the United States; and Lee Meadows, who played many years in the major leagues. Meadows is profiled elsewhere in this book.

Jerome Horner's specialty was Latin but he also was known for his athleticism and coaching ability. Even in his eighties, Horner would go for a swim each day at 6:00 a.m. And in the winter when the ponds froze over, he could be seen ice skating. Also known for his speed in his younger years,

Horner had a very unique way of conducting races. He would fire the starting gun for the hundred-yard dash and then run down to the finish line to judge the winners!

GEORGE C. SHAW

George C. Shaw established the Mary Potter School in 1888. The G.C. Shaw Museum is now located on McClanahan Street in Oxford, and is an excellent resource for information dealing with Shaw's legacy. The museum is in the former house of Shaw, which was built in 1921. Mary Potter School is named for Mrs. Mary Potter, who made generous financial gifts to the school in its formative years. Many graduates of Mary Potter School have gone on to make vital and important contributions to both the state and country.

GEORGIA THOMPSON

Georgia Thompson was born in 1893 in Creedmoor. She was so small her parents started calling her Tiny. After being adopted by Charles Broadwick, she became Tiny Broadwick. In 1908 Tiny, at the age of fifteen, jumped from a hot air balloon. She soon became known as "The Doll Girl" for her diminutive size. In 1913 over sixty thousand people witnessed Tiny become the first woman to parachute from an airplane at Griffith Park in Los Angeles.

Tiny made over eleven hundred jumps in her career. During World War II she served as an advisor to the Aeronautic Corps, and visited many military bases to talk with pilots and parachutists.

In 1978 Broadwick died at the age of eighty-five. She is now buried in Henderson, where her family had moved form Creedmoor.

LUTHER WILKERSON

Luther Wilkerson of Stovall was the first scoutmaster in North Carolina. Wilkerson's Boy Scout troop was chartered in 1911. A popular trip for Wilkerson's troop was to attend reunions of Confederate veterans, where the boys aided and escorted any veteran who needed help. Wilkerson, a jeweler and watch and clock repairman by trade, paid for his troop's finances out of his own pocket. Now buried in the Stovall Baptist Church Cemetery, his tombstone inscription records that he was the first Boy Scoutmaster in North Carolina.

FRANCIS HAYS

This author has turned to the Francis Hays collection in the Richard Thornton Library many times. The collection was compiled by Francis Hays of Oxford, and it includes many books on Granville County history and a plethora of old newspaper clippings.

Hays co-owned Furman and Hays Drugstore, located where the old Hall's Drugstore is now. In 1891 he moved to New York to accept a job as editor of the *Druggists Circular*, from which he retired in 1934. He then moved back to Oxford, and lived in the former Hotel Oxford, which stood on Hillsborough Street. His later years were devoted largely to compiling his historical information on Granville County and writing interesting articles for the *Oxford Public Ledger.*

HARVEY BULLOCK

Harvey Bullock was born in 1921 in Oxford. When his father took a new job three years after Harvey's birth, the Bullock family moved to New York. Harvey came back to the area to attend college at Duke, where he was a high hurdler on the track team and wrote for the campus paper. World War II was raging as Harvey graduated from Duke, and as he said, "Five days after I received my diploma, I was doing pushups at Notre Dame Midshipman School."

Are you a fan of *The Andy Griffith Show*? If so, you can be proud of the fact that Harvey Bullock, born in Oxford, wrote the scripts for over thirty of the shows, including "Opie's Hobo Friend," "The Pickle Story" and "The Loaded Goat." Bullock also wrote scripts for *The Dick Van Dyke Show*, *The Doris Day Show*, *Hogan's Heroes* and *The Love Boat*. Among his movie credits were *Girl Happy*, starring Elvis Presley in 1965, and Donny and Marie Osmond's *Goin' Coconuts* in 1978.

Granville County Hospital

Much credit for this column goes to a previously written pamphlet called "A History of Brantwood Nursing School."

In 1920, local leaders in Granville County recognized the need for a hospital. Doctors Sam Watkins, W.N. Thomas and Jack Bullock decided Oxford was the place for this hospital, and they bought the home of E.H. Hicks, along with several acres of land. The house was altered to meet hospital requirements. One unique addition was the installation of an elevator, which required the passenger to pull the cage up by a rope hand over hand.

Two other smaller houses that were purchased served as the home for Riley Phillips, the hospital's first orderly, and Herbert Faucette, who tended the adjacent farm. The Faucette house soon became the Nurses' Home.

The hospital was given the name Brantwood. The original staff included Dr. Jack Bullock (Surgery), Dr. W.N. Thomas (Anatomy), Dr. Sam Watkins (Obstetrics), R.R. Herring (Materia Medica) and Mae White (Superintendent of Nurses).

Several new doctors joined Brantwood soon after it opened, such as W.L. Taylor, Nat Daniel, Roy Noblin, Rivers Taylor and James Bradsher. Registered Nurses were Kate Herndon, Sophia Sizemore and Grade Sonsburger. Among the nurses who completed their course of study was Helen Liles, who had the highest grade average—a ninety-six.

In 1937 a special bond passed, and with aid from the Public Works Administration, the county started building a new hospital directly in front of Brantwood. On March 21, 1938, Granville Hospital officially opened. Dr. W.N. Thomas, who was most instrumental in getting the grant money for the new facility, laid the first brick.

Pictured is Brantwood Hospital in Oxford in the 1920s.

Granville Hospital in 1938.

The old Brantwood house served as the Nurses' Home until it was destroyed by fire in 1953. The nurses were served their meals in a lovely dining room paneled in solid mahogany. Most of the food consumed in the hospital was grown on the farmland in the back of the building. Martha Hobgood was one of the girls' favorite cooks, especially with her freezer of ice cream on Sundays.

The nurses made $10 per month in the summer and $7.50 in the winter. Uniforms, room and board and laundry were also provided by the hospital. The young ladies worked twelve hours a day with two hours off for study or to take care of personal matters. They remained on call for emergencies at all times. On night duty, they would be required to fire up the furnace in the basement during the winter.

Many additions have been made to Granville Hospital since its opening in 1938. This facility has served our region well, and continues to do so today.

Richard H. Thornton Library

If you walk into my house, you will probably first notice stacks of books on the kitchen table, even next to the kitchen sink of all places. When you sit on my couch you may have to slide a few books or magazines out of the way to make room! Be careful if you look in my bedroom closet—my clothes are few in number compared to the books, which may tumble on your head. My truck is the same. It usually takes me several minutes to remove my books to make room in the passenger seat. When you see my books, you will have no trouble surmising that I love to read.

Several factors contributed to my love of reading. Probably the most important was my mother, Mary Bowling. She has always read, albeit a lot of fiction, as compared to my preferred nonfiction. But I can see her point. After raising me and my six siblings, escaping from the real world for a few moments into a realm of fantasy must have been a relief.

My dad, O.L. Bowling Jr., was not a big reader, but when you have nine mouths to feed three times a day things have a way of taking priority.

And you know how some memories stick with you forever? I still vividly recall one of my grandfathers, Lewis Walker, always pulling out a box of paperback books from under his bed, and telling me to take as many as I wanted. I would be the happiest kid in all of Granville County as I rode home from "papa's" house with books each time I visited him.

I also owe thanks to the Richard Thornton Library in Oxford. As a kid, you could always find me in one of two places if I wasn't working: playing ball or in the library checking out books. I simply could not get enough of Thomas Jefferson, George Washington, Honest Abe and Daniel Boone.

Two quotations come to mind as I write about reading. Socrates said that "to be content with little is to approach the divine." A book in the hands of a

Richard Thornton, *left*, and Robert Frost, *right*, as they visit in Oxford. The woman is Richard Thornton's wife, Nina.

voracious reader is a good analogy. Billy Graham said that good books "will stretch the mind without doing violence to the soul." I think we all know what "good book" Mr. Graham had in mind.

The Thornton Library opened its doors on May 10, 1964. Many people helped in establishing the new library including the Critcher family of the *Oxford Public Ledger*, Tom Johnson, Moo Yancey, Will Hicks, Mrs. Kate Parham, Mrs. Mary Jamieson, Sophronia Cooper, Edith Cannady and many others. Richard Thornton and his wife Nina donated most of the money for the library, so it was decided that the name of this new building should be the Richard H. Thornton Library. Mr. Thornton had accumulated his wealth through shrewd stock investments and his work in the publishing industry.

The impetus for a new library took place in St. Stephen's Episcopal Church. Mr. Thornton was teaching a Bible class on a very rainy morning and only one person showed up: Tom Johnson, editor of *the Oxford Public Ledger*. Thornton told Johnson that Granville County was in need of a new library, and that he would give $75,000 toward its construction if the county could raise another $75,000.

Fundraising then started and the library eventually came to fruition.

Granville County had a library before Thornton Library was built, housed in the old buggy factory building on Williamsboro Street. In fact,

Granville County has the distinction of being the first county in the South to levy a special county library tax.

Many people, including some already mentioned, worked hard to maintain the Granville County Library. Clem Credle, better known for the school that bears his name, C.G. Credle, lent support. W.T. Yancey of Blalock Chevrolet in Oxford loaned the library an automobile to take books to county residents. William Poe and Ben Parham served on the Library Board, along with others. The Oxford Woman's Club started library services in Granville County, striving to improve cultural opportunities for citizens.

Our library has served us well through our history, and continues to do so. I close by quoting Gerald Johnson from his dedication speech for the Thornton Library in 1964:

> *I rejoice that you have a new library because you can use it and, above all, you can enjoy it. "There is no frigate like a book to bear us lands away," sang Emily Dickinson. I know that within these walls, for years and years to come, Oxford people, boys and girls, grandfathers and grandmothers too, without moving from their chairs, will voyage to Smarcand, to Circe's Isle, and the garden of the Hesperides, and so voyaging will look on life and find it brave and splendid.*

Creedmoor

Creedmoor was incorporated in 1905, having previously been known as Creedmore. Joseph Peed served as Creedmoor's first mayor, while the first town commissioners were J.F. Sanderford, Isaac Bullock, S.C. Lyon, Claude Garner and L.H. Longmire. S.C. Lyon was a son of Thomas Lyon, who is generally regarded as the founder of Creedmoor. At one time Lyon owned most of the land around what is now Creedmoor, and in 1886 he applied to the Postal Department for a Creedmoor post office, which was granted. John Harmon served as the first postmaster. In 1888, Lyon sold part of his land to the Durham and Northern Railroad for a track to run through Creedmoor. The old railroad depot building still stands today as a vestige of another era. Linking Creedmoor on this line between Henderson and Durham was a major cause of growth of this Granville County town. Lyon also sold the land for the First Baptist Church, located on Elm Street, in 1895. The present Baptist Church was built in 1950 on Main Street.

Creedmoor is thought to have gotten its name from a traveling lexicographer—what today we would call a dictionary salesman. This man's name was Mr. Creed Moor.

To a large degree, Creedmoor owes its existence to tobacco, just like Oxford, Stem, Stovall and other places in Granville County. Four tobacco warehouses were built in Creedmoor in the early 1900s. In 1906, Jim Netherly and Mr. Cooper built Creedmoor Supply Company, which sold feed, mules, horses, buggies and even some groceries to meet the demands of local farmers. In fact, at one time, Creedmoor was one of the largest tobacco markets in the area, but the farm item for which Creedmoor became nationally known was mules. People came from all over the country to buy and sell mules. Some even referred to Creedmoor affectionately as "Mule Town." G.M. Chappell built a barn that auctioned mules, cows

Hotel Granville in Creedmoor in the 1920s.

and horses from 1938 to 1962. Not everyone had tractors to plow fields, so strong mules between three and four years of age and weighing up to thirteen hundred pounds were needed. Mules, a cross between a horse and a donkey, had smaller feet than horses, so they did not step on tobacco plants as horses did. By 1940, over a half-million dollars were traded in Creedmoor on these pleasant, hardworking animals.

Creedmoor would be transformed into a busy place on mule auction days, just as Oxford became swamped with farmers during tobacco auction days at its warehouse. Hundreds of mules, stacked twenty-four to a boxcar, would arrive by train at the depot on Elm Street. A white horse was used to lead the mules to the barn. Sadly, as farms grew in size and tractors became more affordable, the demand for mules decreased.

Having grown up on a farm myself, I fondly remember our mule Pearl. Pearl was the gentlest creature. I even rode Pearl around Providence, where I grew up, with my friends who were on horses and ponies. Style points didn't matter to me. I felt very safe on my old friend. Of course, carrying my little body (at that time!) probably felt like a vacation to Pearl after pulling trailers of tobacco all day long. Now that I think about it, I almost feel guilty as Pearl probably needed to be resting. At the end of the day in the fields, there would almost be a fistfight among us to determine who would get to ride Pearl back to the barn. The older ones had the good sense to hop on a tractor or truck so they could call it a day sooner. For some strange reason I have always enjoyed watching animals eat, and I can still vividly remember Pearl sucking down an entire bucket of water without pause and consuming huge amounts of hay and corn. I know I must sound like quite an oddball, but this gentle old farm animal gave me as many pleasant memories from my childhood as my human friends did.

Creedmoor High School opened in 1909 at the intersection of Main Street and Highway 56. J.A. Pitts, a graduate of Duke University—then called Trinity College—was the first principal. This school served grades one through twelve until 1963, when white students went to South Granville High School. Hawley School, dedicated in 1937, educated area black students. In 1970, Creedmoor School, at that time serving grades one through eight, burned down.

During World War II, downtown Creedmoor became a booming place. Soldiers from nearby Camp Butner would come to town on nights off to relax and have a good time. There was a bowling alley and the Granville Theatre was where the Creedmoor Drugstore is today. A United Service Organization (USO) was in the building where the *Butner-Creedmoor News* is now located on Main Street.

Creedmoor today is still a "small town," but it is a town that is growing while retaining its link to the past. The old First National Bank building has been refurbished, Harry Coleman has his farm museum on the second floor of the newspaper building and there are antique shops downtown. Creedmoor is a proud part of Granville County history and, to its residents, a good place to call home.

An Oxford Boy
Makes the Big Leagues

This is a story about Lee Meadows, not to be confused with Ed Meadows, the football player. Lee was one of the best major league baseball pitchers of the 1910s and 1920s.

Lee Meadows was born in Oxford in 1894 and attended Horner Military School in Oxford where, unsurprisingly, he was a star baseball player. Like most people in and around Oxford in those days, Lee worked in tobacco. In an interview in 1916, after reaching the big leagues, he said, "I always liked to hang around tobacco warehouses in Oxford when I was a youngster, and I still have the fever." He also enjoyed hunting as a young man, and next to baseball, these were his two favorite activities for the rest of his life. A word of warning was in order, however, if you were a hunting partner of young Lee's or if you faced him on the mound as a batter. You needed to make sure he had his "specs" on. "I can't tell a cat from an elephant at twelve feet without my specs," said Meadows.

Lee's glasses won him fame. He became the first major leaguer to wear glasses after making the St. Louis Cardinals in 1915. He had many nicknames, among them "Specs" Meadows, the "Four-Eyed Pitcher" and the "Eye-Glassed Twirler." At this time, wearing glasses was thought to be a severe handicap for an athlete, and of course, this was before the age of contact lenses. The first couple of years of his big league career, Lee was better known for his glasses than for his pitching prowess. A baseball magazine had this to say in 1915: "Eye-glassed men everywhere are perking up and taking heart, and big league managers are being flooded with letters from aspiring pitchers who wear monocles."

Despite his glasses, Meadows became one of the best hurlers of his era. He was six feet tall and weighed 190 pounds, a size which was big at the

Lee Meadows of Oxford won 188 games as a pitcher in the major leagues.

time. He played for St. Louis from 1915–1919, for the Philadelphia Phillies from 1920–1923 and for the Pittsburgh Pirates from 1924–1928. He was the opening game pitcher in both the 1925 and 1927 World Series and won twenty games in 1926. He finished his career with 188 wins and with a very good 3.38 ERA (Earned Run Average). Among those 188 wins were forty shutouts. While with the Pirates, Lee discussed his thoughts on hitters:

I have been asked if certain hitters bother me when I am obliged to face them. They do not. I don't really care what a batter does when he's in the box. He can dance a clog dance as much as he pleases and wiggle his bat in any manner that suits his convenience. I'm rather glad to have him cut up because he may give me a hint on what to throw him.

After his playing days, Meadows stayed in baseball, becoming manager of the Deland Reds minor league team in Florida, and later served as president of the Daytona Beach Knothole Gang team.

A Few Good Poems

Wallace Wade was a great football coach at Duke University, where he took the Blue Devils to several Rose Bowls. Coach Wade also led Alabama to three national titles. I have written a biography of Coach Wade, called *Wallace Wade: Championship Years at Alabama and Duke.*

Thad Stem of Oxford was a student at Duke in the 1930s when Coach Wade was among the most successful coaches in the nation. Stem wrote the following poem about Coach Wade.

A Legend At Duke

In all the days of future years,
his name and fame will shine,
Our brilliant, Iron Colonel,
Of our old Blue Devil line.

And men will tell their children,
although other memories fade,
how they played for the
Mighty Dukes of Durham
And 'old man' Wallace Wade.

The Opera House once held plays, lectures and other cultural events from its Williamsboro Street location in Oxford.

Earle Hunt, an Oxford High School graduate, wrote this poem that is so timely today as the Iraq War rages on:

To our Soldier Boys

Go forth! Go forth' cross the ocean deep,
Or the desert far and wide!
Though loved ones you leave behind may weep,
Just think of your country's pride.
Go fight for the right of the U.S.A.!
May our country forever live!
Each fight like a man as brave as you can,
If even your life you must give.

Come back, come back to the U.S.A.!
When the fierce war times are o'er.
You'll be welcomed again to your old home town
As you've never been welcomed before.
Come back with your lives to your children and wives,
To your sisters and brothers return.
Your fathers will cheer, when your brave deeds they hear,
And dear mothers' love will still burn

Hotel Oxford once stood proudly in downtown Oxford.

Hillsboro Street in the 1940s. *Photo courtesy of Granville County Historical Society Museum.*

Thad Stem of Oxford wrote this poem with other wars in mind, but it is appropriate for now with the United States at war in Iraq:

The Spirit of Liberty Says

I saw the trees of Oxford
As I was passing by,
I saw the fields of Granville
Against the Carolina sky.
I saw the boys with balls and bats,
So merrily at their play,
But when there came the call to arms
They put their toys away.
Listen ye people of Oxford Town:
Hear the distant bugle call?
Hear their steadfast voices resound
Through Time's long, hallowed hall:
Kings Mountain, Yorktown, Gettysburg,
The Argonne and San Juan Hill;
Bellicourt, Flanders, Salerno,
The Solomans and Bourgainville.
God rest you Granville Gentlemen
Who laid your good lives down,
God rest you in a fairer place
Than even Oxford Town.

A view of College Street in Oxford in the 1940s. *Photo courtesy of Granville County Historical Society Museum.*

A view of Williamsboro Street in Oxford around 1940.

Pat Colenda, an archivist at Oxford's Masonic Home for Children, wrote this poem about Oxford:

Our Town

Beautiful old homes overlooking shady streets,
Where the branches of old trees rustle as they meet.
There's a feeling of forever as if time will not let go,
An intertwining past and present that ever will be so.

Buildings that through the years have stood the test of time,
Churches with steeples soaring and ivy creeps and climbs.
Schools ever feeding the minds of our town's youth,
Growing minds seeking for wisdom and truth.

In the glory of color the fall season is here,
In our little town a special time of year.
The mist in the morning and chill in the night,
Beautiful days all golden and bright.

In the cold of the winter—the beauty of snow,
The season of moisture to make things grow.
The coming alive in the spring of our town,
When flowers and Dogwood bloom all around.

The planting and growing and tilling the sod,
The music and laughter and worship of God.
The joy of just being a part of a place
Filled with such beauty, warmth, charm and grace.

Owen Motor Company in Oxford.

Participant in the Hoover Car Parade in Oxford.

A College in Oxford

Oxford Female College started in 1851. Its purpose was to help young ladies to "cultivate habits of accurate and ready observation, develop the reason powers, improve the taste and fancy and store the mind with useful knowledge."

By 1858, there were ninety-two ladies attending Oxford Female College, with eighty-one from North Carolina, five from Virginia, two from Tennessee, two from Mississippi and two from Texas. Courses were offered in ethics, metaphysics, literature, Latin, French, music, drawing and painting and embroidery. The goal of the educational process was summed up by the following:

> *At one end goes in a school girl,*
> *Rough and rude and void of culture;*
> *From the other comes a lady,*
> *A wise and well-accomplished woman.*

The young ladies were expected to wear a uniform of "bonnet trimmed with blue, cloak and dress of blue merino, for winter, and for summer a bonnet trimmed with pink, and dresses of solid pink and white." Among the numerous offenses: sitting or standing in an unbecoming position, leaving the premises without permission and receiving the visits or attentions of young gentlemen, or in any way corresponding with them.

In 1880 Franklin Hobgood became president of the Oxford Female College, and stayed in this position until 1924. Rules remained strict during Hobgood's tenure. Students were required to write home once a week and were prohibited from eating at "unseasonable hours."

Part of the Oxford College Campus.

The Oxford College tennis team in 1913.

On January 18, 1904, at 8:00 a.m., the frame building of the college was destroyed by a fire. Four new buildings were built, one of which still stands today.

President Hobgood died in 1924, and the school closed permanently the next year. The schools and places of business in Oxford closed on the day of Hobgood's funeral, and quiet as death seemed the streets through which passed the long funeral cortege out to Elmwood Cemetery from the college chapel.

T.G. Stem, mayor of Oxford at the time of Hobgood's death in 1924, gave a moving address to an overflow crowd in the Oxford Baptist Church for a memorial service. Stem said:

> [Hobgood] *was endowed with the happy faculty of making those with whom he came in contact believe in themselves, and possessed the art of drawing out the very best in those with whom he was associated. Our loss is great and our sorrow intense, but in the consciousness of the mighty works he wrought and the glorious life he lived, and in the lingering radiance of his unbounded love and unstinted service we can indeed let gladness mingle with our tears.*

The Hester Family Tragedy

August 10, 1937, is a date that will always be remembered in Creedmoor, North Carolina. On this day many years ago, tragedy visited this small farming community.

Clyde Hester married Edgar Hester and she would eventually give birth to nine children. Their firstborn was Claresse, who came into the world in 1904. Claresse developed rheumatism and suffered most of her life before dying at the age of seven in 1911. A local reporter wrote about her funeral:

> *Her little body was laid to rest in Creedmoor Cemetery amid a large throng who will ever feel and miss her sweet little face. But oh, what joy to think of her "Safe in the arms of Jesus, Safe on his gentle breast."*

Mrs. Hester endured, leaning on her devout Christian faith. Soon more sadness came her way. Another daughter, Mildred, died three years later at the tender age of five. In 1924, another daughter, who bore her mother's name of Clyde, died at the age of eighteen. Three daughters lost within thirteen years, all taken before reaching womanhood. Clyde was distraught with sorrow, as any mother would be. She turned for sustenance to her beloved God, expressing her gratitude for still having her husband and six other children. As she had read in her Bible many times, "The Lord giveth and the Lord taketh away, blessed be the name of the Lord." Clyde and Edgar devoted their attention to their remaining children. Maurice, Vivian, Mary, Edith, Annie and Joe gave them much pleasure.

By 1937, Maurice was a graduate of East Carolina Teacher's College and was a teacher in the fourth grade at Stem School. Vivian had recently completed a business course in Raleigh and was anticipating the day she could begin stenographic work. Mary had just graduated from Creedmoor

High School, while Edith was a junior at the same school. These young ladies were greatly loved in the community. They were all active in the community's social and religious life. At home they were so devoted to one another that they were almost inseparable.

Just like thousands of other families in the Piedmont section of North Carolina, Edgar and Clyde Hester rose from bed on August 10, 1937, to harvest another field of tobacco. Most families in Granville County, of which Creedmoor is a part, made their living from this staple crop. It was a life of hard work, but the Hesters were successful at it. Today, like so many other days, the tobacco would be harvested as a family affair. This day, which began with bright sunshine and optimism, sadly would end with the Carolina blue sky turning into a dark, vicious killer.

Maurice, Vivian, Mary, Edith and Joe were in the tobacco fields helping with the crop. Annie was away from home working elsewhere. Around 4:00 p.m., thick black clouds appeared and a slight gust of wind stirred the hot, dry dust of the field. A few drops of rain fell from the sky, and before long torrents of water were falling on the heads of the Hester children, their father Edgar, Roy Mangum and Eugene Rogers. Joe and the three other men went to a nearby wagon to prepare some shelter. The four young Hester girls huddled together under guano sacks with their arms around each other. Suddenly, without warning, a lightning bolt shot from the ominous sky, striking the Hester girls. They died as they so lovingly lived—together. One lightning bolt and four lay dead.

After hearing the terrible news, Clyde again, as always, showed her courageous spirit. She had now lost seven daughters in the past twenty-six years, none living beyond the age of twenty-five. But Clyde continued to remain strong, often quoting the Bible: "Though you slay me, I will still serve you. The Lord knows what is best."

The funeral was conducted at the Creedmoor Baptist Church by the Reverend S.L. Morgan. A large crowd was expected, but people came in such numbers that more than a thousand had to stand outside the church and listen to the service through amplifiers. Places of business in town closed for the day. Inside the church, the four white caskets stood before high banks of flowers. Later the four girls were laid to rest side by side in one large grave. They lived together, died together and justly were buried together. Their mother, of such strong faith, believed all four would soon be together in heaven.

Seven precious girls, all taken at a tender age, all called to heaven. But death came calling to Clyde Hester again. On the morning of July 10, 1941, Clyde heard an explosion in an upstairs bedroom. She ran to the room, there finding Edgar, her husband, dead from a self-inflicted shotgun blast. Edgar had been tortured by the deaths of his young daughters, and was also experiencing bad health himself. When a couple of neighbors arrived at the Hester house, they could hear through the open windows someone alternately quoting scripture and singing hymns. As they reached the upstairs bedroom, they found Clyde Hester cleaning up the blood from her husband. It was she, again relying on her faith in God, who was now praising his name.

Mrs. Clyde Hester would live on. Popularly regarded as "the best Christian in town," she remained a good mother to her two remaining children. Annie lived to be eighty-one and Joe died in 2000. Clyde passed away in 1964. This lady endured more pain and sorrow than anyone should have to. She had choices as death visited her family. She could have become bitter and lost faith in God. But Clyde Hester was too strong a lady to be defeated. Second Timothy 2:3 says, "Thou therefore endure hardness, as a good soldier of Jesus Christ." The town of Creedmoor was truly graced by the presence of a good soldier, Clyde Hester. Her life enriched all Granville Countians and continues to be an example to this day. I end with a section of a poem titled "The Rose Still Grows Beyond the Wall."

Shall claim of death cause us to grieve,
And make our courage faint or fail?
Nay! Let us faith and hope receive:
The rose still grows beyond the wall.

Scattering fragrance far and wide,
Just as it did in days of yore,
Just as it did on the other side,
Just as it will forevermore!

About the Author

Lewis Bowling teaches in the physical education departments at North Carolina Central University and Duke University in Durham, North Carolina. He has authored four history books on his native Granville County, and writes a history column called "Looking Back" for the *Oxford Public Ledger*. Bowling has also authored *Wallace Wade: Championship Years at Alabama and Duke* and *Resistance Training: The Total Approach,* and is a contributing author to *Lifetime Physical Fitness*. Additionally, he writes a weekly fitness column for the *Durham Herald-Sun*. Contact Lewis at lewis_bowling@yahoo.com or (919) 477-7046 for comments.

Visit us at
www.historypress.net